Ipswich
The War Years

First published in 2005 by: First Edition Limited,
32 Stamford Street, Altrincham, Cheshire, WA14 1EY
in conjunction with
Evening Star, Ipswich, Suffolk.

ISBN: 1-84547-092-3

Contents

.

Shopping was a very different experience during the 1930s and 40s than it is today. Instead of supermarkets stacked with endless products, Ipswich residents visited a number of different shops to get their goods. This images shows a busy Westgate Street in central Ipswich in 1949.

Introduction

Kindred Spirits was born in a five minute meeting I had with Nigel Pickover, the editor of the Evening Star, in August 2000. I was then the newspapers picture editor and had for over a decade taken a keen interest in all the "stray" vintage photographic images there were around recording the Ipswich areas past.

A popular column, which was published in the Evening Star under the heading of "The Way We Were" in the 1970's and 80's was to return in some form as readers showed a keen interest in nostalgia.

"You write it" said Nigel. I have always described myself as a photographer. This is the side of journalism I had worked in then for over thirty years. A photographer write? I could hear feature writers falling off their chairs! I had the idea that it should be the readers memories, not my own. I set the ball rolling with a few ideas and asked for readers own stories.

I thought at best this could run for a few months before running dry, but now over five years later "Kindred Spirits" is still bringing great human interest stories from readers.

The facts and figures of local history are well documented. We know when important buildings were constructed, how many air raids and tragic deaths there were during World War Two, when schools were built and what they cost. I think it is important also to hear the human stories to bring the history alive.

Some vivid and in some ways frightening stories have come from readers who spent their childhood in orphanages. The strict Victorian attitude seems to have continued through to the 1930's and '40's where innocent children were treated like criminals just because they had lost their parents.

For those of us born after the Second World War it is hard to imagine your home town being a target for German bombers, but Ipswich with its engineering factories turning out munitions, the rail link, airport and dock put the town on the list for air raids.

The town suffered over fifty attacks from the air. The first was on the night of 21/22 June 1940 and the last on 4 March 1945. The death toll was 53 with 164 seriously injured, 206 houses were totally destroyed, 766 seriously damaged, but repairable and 10,400 slightly damaged. There were 1,165 air raid alerts to worry residents. Over sixty years later dramatic stories of the war period are being told through the weekly "Kindred Spirits" pages in the Evening Star. With bombs raining down from the sky school children had to run to hastily built shelters to continue lessons. Most young men were torn from their jobs and families and women had to take over traditional male jobs like engineering and keeping the buses running.

All of these areas have provided a rich vane of fascinating human stories, some sad, some funny, but hearing it first hand brings history alive.

Life in the poor housing close to the town centre was harsh. Being moved from the bad housing with gas lamps to new council housing in the 1930s is still clear in peoples memory. As children they had for the first time electric lights to switch on and off at will. Readers recall using the light switches for hours, like a new toy, when they first moved in.

Photographs are often tucked away in cupboards and drawers and the idea evolved that I, with my photographic knowledge, could create a small archive. So many negatives and prints of events around the town are thrown away in house clearance after a family death for example. The dusty old box of photographs are well down in the list of important things to do at such a time, but often among the family holiday snaps there is the only surviving image of a street party, or the corner shop run by granddad.

Given the chance I copy the photograph or print the negatives and it is amazing the response that comes even from the oldest of images once they are published. Readers look at a photograph of a Victory in Europe or Victory in Japan street party taken in 1945 and can name most of the faces featured. School groups from the 1930s are also identified in the same way. The photographs are from a time when families lived in tight little neighbourhood communities where a lifetime was spent together.

This book has brought together some of the memories of Ipswich. It is a chance to relive life in the town in one of the more dramatic periods. It brings together memories in a form that will keep forever.

I hope you enjoy this look back brought to you with many thanks to the wonderful folk who took the time to recall their lives in Ipswich all those years ago.

David Kindred 2005.

This image shows Ipswich docks from the Gasworks around 1930

Around Ipswich

The history of Ipswich goes back to the seventh century. The town grew up because of the crossing of the river at Stoke Bridge. It was the first point on the river from the coast where it was narrow enough for a bridge to be built. The town was originally known as Gipeswic. The port has always been an important part of the town. It was a great vision when the Victorians decided to build the then largest wet dock in the land by creating 33 acres of enclosed water by damming the River Orwell and creating New Cut to take the tidal flow of the river past their new venture. This area has seen a recent transition from cargo trade to a leisure area full of pleasure craft and is increasingly surrounded by apartments hotels and restaurants in an area now known as the Waterfront.

Home Medics

Pills and potions are today available to us off the shelf. There was a time when every family had its own ideas of what would work best to return a member to fitness. Tallow fat was rubbed on children's chests. It came from a slaughterhouse mainly from cattle and was also used to make candles and soap. Camphor cubes and strange brews from the local chemist shop were the only way most could afford medicine in a time before a National Health Service.

Ninety-four-year old Amelia Cobb, of Felix Road, Ipswich, told us of how medicine was in her home when she was a child. Amelia recalls visiting the tannery in Tanners Lane to collect fat.

"My mother sent me to the tannery to buy three penny worth of fat in a Golden Syrup tin, I was about seven to eight years old, which would be 1916 or 1917. The Tallow fat was used by mother to rub on the chests of us children in the winter to prevent us getting a chesty cold. I believe the fat was only used for two winters as my mother found another cure less smelly, Camphor Cubes. These were crushed and put into tiny cloth bags that my mother made and they were stitched on to our bodices. The smell from them was not as strong as Camphor Balls."

"Mother also made our cough mixture. Two of the ingredients I remember were

Amelia Cobb recalls visiting Wiggins Chemist shop in St Matthews Street to get ingredients for her mother's homemade medicine. The shop is second on the left. This picture is from the 1950s. The street changed very little until the redevelopment of the area in the mid 1960s.

ABOVE Elephants were part of the Silver Jubilee procession in Westgate Street, Ipswich 6 May 1935. These photographs were taken by keen armature photographer "Charlie" Girling, a member of the Ipswich Photographic Society.

RIGHT This images shows the view from a front garden of one of the terraced houses at the bottom of Bishops Hill, Ipswich, 26 June 1930. The Prince of Wales had passed by en route to visit the nearby Ransomes Sims and Jefferies engineering works after flying into Ipswich Airport from Northolt. This view is looking towards Fore Hamlet with Myrtle Road off to the left.

Spanish Liquorice which I used to get from Wiggins the Chemist at the corner of Berners Street and St Matthews Street, Ipswich and some aniseed which I had to get from the seed shop in Princes Street."

"In the spring my mother gave us Lime Sulphur tablets every other night for a week. This was my mother said, "To clear the blood".

There was the Friday night Beecham's Pill we used to be given occasionally. Also if one of us had a nasty cold, to prevent the rest of us catching it, mother would boil a saucepan of cut up onions and we were all sent to bed early and given a bowl of hot onion soup, it did the trick. My mother cured many of our ills and we all seemed to thrive."

A trade union march in Grove Lane, Ipswich in around 1932. This view from Alexander Park has a Walls ice cream seller in the foreground with the advertising slogan "Stop Me and Buy One". The leading banner behind the brass band was for the National Union of Railwaymen.

The black line on the wall shows the level the flood water reached in this Sedan Street, Ipswich home in January 1939. Sedan Street was off Princes Street close to the junction of Portman Road. The street was lost to mid-1960s redevelopment.

The Great Flood of 1939

It all started on the morning of 26 January 1939 when torrential rain fell like a monsoon onto a layer of snow. By Thursday morning the Gipping Valley was awash with farmland, villages and homes for miles under several feet of water.

Rail lines were damaged, roads were impassable, and phone communication was in chaos. At Bramford the road bridge over the Gipping collapsed.

It was in Ipswich though where the full force of the floodwater was to be felt. On the Wednesday 2.13 inches of rain fell with water pouring from the higher parts of town. The lower parts around the Princes Street area close to the river were in serious trouble.

Families were trapped in upstairs rooms most with no heat, food or light. One family had only moved into their house in Princes Street on the Monday and was flooded out by the Thursday, never to return.

The way in which the tragedy was reported in the Star at the time illustrates how reporting styles have changed since. It's all a bit "Chin up, keep smiling and stiff upper lip. The report said, "The only aspect of cheerfulness was the amazing fortitude and good humour with which people faced their ill fortune. Families in upper rooms leaned from their bedrooms, joking in philosophical fashion with rescue parties bringing food and water by boat."

"Organisations and institutions in Ipswich assisted in finding accommodation for flood victims, a soup kitchen was opened and convoys of Territorial Army lorries and vans took children to school and men and woman to work."

Portman Road from near Princes Street. On the left is Ipswich Town Football Club who were then in the Third Division. Not surprisingly the match with Reading due that day was postponed.

ABOVE January 1939. A bus makes its way through the flood water in Bridge Street while vehicles and drivers wait their turn on Stoke Bridge. The great flood affected many people and will be long remembered.

ABOVE Residents gathered in Princes Street to view the damage. This was around 48 hours after the flood hit and the water level had dropped back. This picture was taken between Cecilia Street and Chalon Street. On the left is Mrs M Knights tobacconists shop and in the centre Frank Medcalf hairdressers.

LEFT Boys keep their feet dry in Princess Street after the flood.

Joe Everett of Robin Drive, Ipswich lived with his parents in Sedan Street, which was of Princes Street close to the junction with Portman Road.

Joe said. "When the River Gipping burst its banks at Stowmarket all the water came this way and was running back into the River Orwell at Stoke Bridge. The main cause of the river bursting its banks was because the Lock Gates at West End Road were the old wooden, manually operated gates which hadn't been operated for so long. This caused the River Gipping to overflow because they couldn't be opened."

"I lived with my parents at number nine, and so was

involved in this awful experience. The water entered our house on the Thursday afternoon and we were marooned upstairs until about 5pm on the Saturday with the water halfway up the stairs at times."

"In our house was my mother, sister, sister-in-law, brother-in-law, a niece and nephew with no light, no heat and no food. At the bottom of our street, in Cardinal Street, was John Woods Haulage Contractors Yard, which had double gates with his name etc painted on them. We could judge the depth of water by the lettering covered by the water and we were very relieved when we could see the water going down."

"By Saturday evening the water had subsided enough so that Princes Street, which was higher than our street, was dry. We still had about a foot of water in our house

With the rise of the tide during the afternoon on January 26 1930, the River Gipping overflowed its banks and millions of gallons of water poured into the lower-lying portions of the town. Princes Street, the main thoroughfare between Ipswich Railway Station and the Cornhill, became a miniature river and many vehicles were left stranded by the water.

and so to get out we had to call a policeman, who was patrolling Princes Street and wearing waders. He came and stood at the foot of our stairs so we would each climb on his back and he carried us up to Princes Street. We stayed the night with my brother who lived in Gippeswyk Road."

"On the Friday morning the Salvation Army rowed up our street in a boat with jugs of hot soup. We tied scarves together to hang out of the bedroom window so they could tie a jug of soup on the end, which we hauled up inside and were very glad of it."

"On the Monday morning the Rev Green, who was the

vicar of St Nicholas Church and had started a Relief Fund, came round and asked if we needed anything. I told him I had no shoes and he gave me a note to take to Prices Shoe Shop at the corner of Tacket Street and they gave me a pair of shoes."

"On the Sunday morning my mother was anxious to get back to our home, so I went with her and when we got to the top of our street the water had gone. When we entered our house where the water had been there as a layer of black mud and as you walked across the floor you were walking on cutlery, shoes etc that were covered in mud because some of the furniture had overturned and drawers

Crowds gathered to watch as families trapped by the flood were rescued from their homes. The water left huge damage in its wake. Hundreds of homes were ruined by the flood.

LEFT This wonderful image of Alderman Road shows the extent to which flooding affected Ipswich. These people are having to use a boat in order to moved around!

and cupboards were empty."

"We managed to salvage a bucket and a broom and there was still mains water so we washed the mud into a corner and then sifted through it with our hands to find various items in the mud. We managed to swill the mud off the three-piece suite and carpet and drag them out into the street where the council took them away in a lorry."

"I was employed as an engine cleaner on the railway and had to go away to work but my parents lived with my brother for about six months. During this time my mother would go to our house each day and light fires and clean up so they could eventually move back to 9 Sedan Street."

Janet Smith of Salehurst Road, Ipswich was told as a child of the disasters, which struck her grandmother in local floods. Janet lived with her grandmother and uncle in Metz Street from the age of five after the 1939 flood.

Janet said. "Although I didn't live in Ipswich at the time my Grandmother and Uncle told me all about it. They lived in Metz Street, I moved to live with them after my mother died."

"My Grandma was found in the midst of the mud and slime clearing her sewing machine which was her pride and joy. They had to burn all the family photos and personal items as there was disease in the flood water."

Water Supplies

Water was not only used for baths and washing. This extraordinary photograph of police officers swimming in full uniform at the Stoke Bathing Place, Ipswich during a training session in the early 1930s. Stoke Bathing Place was an open air pool. It was little more than a walled of area of the River Orwell with changing huts. This picture was donated by Norma Keeble and includes her father PC Walter Jones (top centre).

"I won't be long, I am just going to the Bumby" or "I am just going to the stream to get more water". Not something you will hear said in homes today.

The "Bumby" was a Suffolk expression for the outside

toilet, used by most homes outside the town (and many in the town) for those who grew up before the Second World War.

Eric Peck, of Austin Street, Ipswich revealed some of the memories of his life in

Freston from the 1930s.

"My father was a carpenter in the building trade and in 1934 there was a shortage of work and to save on expenditure we moved out of Ipswich to The Thatched Cottage, The Strand, Wherstead, at the bottom of Freston Hill."

"I was seven at the time. It was a two up two down with a wash house at the back. There was no electricity, gas or water laid on. All lighting came from paraffin oil lamps or candles, cooking and only heating came from an old cooking range in the living room. How mum coped with the cooking I do not know."

"Depending which way the wind was blowing, the fire would either burn away and over heat, or not give out any heat at all. Mum worked on the farm and it was my job to light the fire and make sure that it was ready to start cooking when she got home. I also had to go to the farm to get the milk."

"The radio was powered by two large batteries and a accumulator which had to be recharged every week."

"The toilet of course was outside (we called it a "bumby") and dad had to empty it at least once a week and bury the contents in the garden."

"The only water supply was from the stream at the bottom of Freston Hill (it's still there). Dad would walk the 200 yards with two pails (buckets) every morning before going to work and then again in the evening if there wasn't enough to last until morning."

"Every Sunday morning he would trek backwards and forwards with two pails until he had filled the copper and water butts with enough water for mum to do the weekly wash. This was fine in the summer as the ground was firm, but in the wintertime it was always very muddy and one day dad lost a "wellie"."

"One problem was if there were cattle on the meadows further up stream, this was also their supply of drinking water and of course they walk into the stream to drink and stirred up the mud so much that sometimes it took a couple of hours to run clear. The tide was another problem, but this you could time."

"Shopping was done once a week in town and mum usually did this on Saturdays. We did have a small van call on Monday with paraffin oil and soap."

Mrs Pearle Scott from New South Wales, Australia, sent memories of the Stoke area of Ipswich and what hard work wash day was before washing machines.

"I was born in Austin Street in 1927 and remember the shrimp man selling fresh Harwich Shrimps, the ferry across New Cut and Stoke Bathing Place."

"My father and some friends started the Stoke Bathing Place Yacht Club in the 30s and used to have a regatta. There was a race from Stoke Bathing Place to the swimming pool at West End, the swimmers were accompanied by dingys and also the rowing club had races."

"In the summer we went down to Pin Mill for the weekends and for a week to Levington Creek. We thought it was wonderful."

"When I look back it was a hard life. Washing day always stands out in my memory. Mother lighting the copper fire in the kitchen, hauling buckets of water and boiling the whites, then blueing them and starching, it was a day's work. When I came home from school for lunch I had to help mother fold the sheets and turn the handle on the mangle, then if they were dry, they were all ironed, it was an all day job and sheets where changed every week. Front doorsteps whitened and knobs and knockers were polished."

"I went to Wherstead Road School and Luther Road School when it opened, then to the Central Senior Girls School in Bolton Lane."

"I joined the WRNS in 1945 and my last two years

Stoke Bridge, Ipswich

where spent at HMS Ganges. I met my husband there and was married in St Peter's Church, Ipswich in 1948. My husband joined the East Suffolk Police, and was stationed at Lowestoft, Sweffling, Saxmundham and Eyke, then the last 10 years as section sergeant at Baylham, his name was Raymond Scott. Then we bought a house in Fountains Road, so I returned to Stoke."

"Looking back to my childhood, although by today's standards we were happy, times hold no comparison to today, everyone knew everyone, and through the Second World War all helped one another."

Stoke Bridge, Ipswich from St Peters Dock. This bridge was opened in 1925 replacing an iron bridge built in 1818, which had replaced a bridge washed away by floods. On the right behind the masts of the barges are the premises of British Fermentation Products Ltd, yeast manufacturers. The skate board park is now on that site.

Starting Out In Work

Stoke is an area of Ipswich rich with memories of the village like atmosphere of this part of town, before Large areas were demolished as the road system changed and large engineering companies like Ransomes and Rapier and Cocksedge Ltd closed. Norman Quantrall of Lower Holbrook worked at the Co-op in Vernon Street.

Norman said, "When I left school at the end of July 1939 I applied for and was granted an interview with Mr. Wheeler the grocery supervisor who told me to report to Vernon Street grocery store. It was on Monday morning 31 July 1939 I first met Harry Wyatt the manager "what's your name lad", "where do you live" "what's your father's name"? "I used to walk to school with him". It transpired that he was brought up in Lower Holbrook like me and he lived at that time in a cottage, long ago demolished, right on the border of Lower Holbrook and Harkstead."

"My first job was cleaning brass scales but within an hour the large covered lorry arrived from the Paul's Road depot with the weekly supplies to unload. The sides of bacon and crates of New Zealand cheeses were taken down to the cellar via a trap door in the middle of the shop. The dry goods were stored in two warehouses out back and the flour and animal feed went up an outside stairs to the first floor bins that funnelled down to the backroom of the shop ready for weighing up as required."

"After lunch it was down to the cellar to skin the cheeses. The only female staff at that time was Miss Doris Berry and a junior in the cash desk, which was slightly raised, the terminal for the overhead wires that carried the cups containing the cash and the dividend cheques. As a warehouse boy much of my time was spent delivering orders by trade bike and each morning, going to the office in Carr Street with paper work and collecting medication from the central chemists for customers ordered the previous day."

"He was one of the most cheerful work mates one could wish for, as I found out a few months after arriving when I was promoted into the shop as most of the men had gone off to war and young women took their places. In those days on the provision counter the butter was weighed on suspended scales using two wooden tools. It was cut and pat into shape before wrapping. Wednesday afternoons and Sundays the young staff did fire watching duty with the older members doing the nights."

"All the sugar was weighted and bagged by hand as well as the dried fruit, 4oz. wrapped in a single sheet made into a cone and 8oz. wrapped flat like a bar of chocolate. I left the Co-op in March 1942 and opened a wet fish shop until I went into the forces a year later."

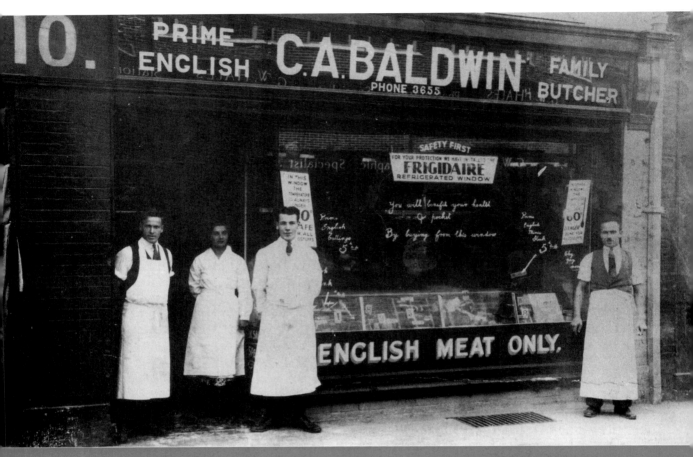

Charles Baldwin (right) outside his butchers shop at 8 Tacket Street, Ipswich in the 1930s. Mr Baldwin had the first refrigerated window display in Ipswich. Mrs Nora Baldwin is in the shop doorway with the shop's two assistants.

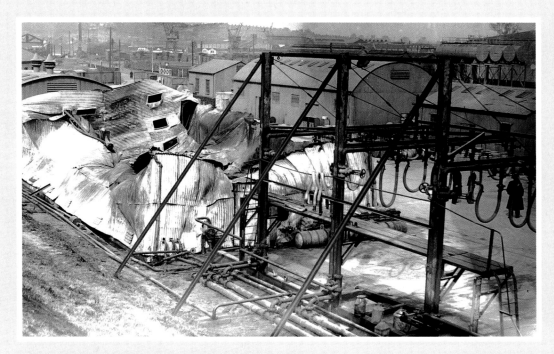

A fuel dump at Cliff Quay was amongst the targets of a German Air Raid of 9/10th of April 1941.

Bombing

Ipswich was targeted by German bombers during World War Two. The town with its dock, rail links, airport and engineering works so close to the east coast was a relatively easy target for raiders. The town had suffered brief bombing raids during World War One as massive Zeppelins flew over the town with the crew dropping incendiary bombs but nothing could have prepared the residents of Ipswich for the horrors which would rain from the sky during the Second World War.

The first bombs fell early in the war when on the night of 21 June 1940 three people were killed in a house in Dale Hall Lane. Between then and 4 March 1945, when nine people were killed in Seymour Road, Ipswich suffered 55 air raids. Fifty three people were killed and 164 seriously injured.

Bombs Away

TOP Damaged buildings close to the dock are show here. They were hit in the air raid of 9/10 April 1941. The German Air Force made frequent raids into Ipswich, and many hundreds of buildings were damaged, with the sad loss of life. On the night of 9/10 April 1941 around 13 high explosive bombs were dropped on the dock area of Ipswich. In the raid the fire service boat was sunk and a crew member, P/O Clements was killed. Here the boat is being raised. In the right background is the Old Custom House.

Mrs L King of Landseer Road, Ipswich, recalls being evacuated when her home was hit in an air raid. Mrs King said. "My house was bombed in June 1940, there were three houses hit that night. Eight children were all down in the shelter. My mum and dad and new baby were in the house when it was hit. We went to Holywells Mansion for two days till we were re-housed. We came back to Gainsborough after about two years and moved into the house next door. We needed to be in that part of town as my dad was a boatman at the docks and had to go out when he heard ships blowing their hooters as they sailed up the River Orwell."

"We came from Upper Orwell Courts where eight children and my mum and dad lived in a one up and one down little house, shared toilet and tap. We moved to Gainsborough to a new house, it seemed like a mansion to us then."

Beryl Willson (nee Garrard) of Bennett Road, Ipswich, remembers the Anderson shelter built in her back garden while other members of the family used a Morrison shelter Beryl said. "I lived in Bennett Road, but sometimes my mum, brother David and myself, went to stay for the weekend with my Auntie Floss and her son Eric in Queensgate

The crew of the fireboat, which was sunk by a bomb in April 1941. In the centre is P/O Clements who was killed in the raid.

Drive. Our Dads being away in the forces. We had an Anderson shelter in our back garden, but Auntie had a Morrison shelter in her back room."

"When we visited them, they slept on a mattress inside the shelter and we slept on a mattress on top of the shelter. When there was a raid on, we would all get inside the shelter. Being children we thought it was fun!"

"One weekend when we were there, we missed the worst attack in our home area, when incendiary bombs were dropped on some bungalows in Brockley Crescent and down the centre of Bennett Road. Fortunately our house was not hit. I still live in that same house where we

moved to the day before war was declared in 1939."

"One day I remember standing outside our Anderson shelter watching two German airmen with guns firing, floating down on parachutes. They landed on Bramford Road bridge. Another time we watched a "Doodlebug" going along, hoping it would not drop near us. It eventually hit the Lowestoft area. I still have my gas mask in its original box with string for a shoulder strap!"

Tom Scrivener of, Heron Road, Ipswich remembers one of the air raids on Ipswich Dock

"I have memories of the air raid on Ipswich docks, of February 1941. My neighbour and school friend at the time Ronny Wilson, was walking along Upper Orwell Street (The Wash). We were about level with the back of the old fire station, which was in Bond

Street, when we saw this aircraft very low over the shops heading towards the dock area. The next thing was a loud bang with others to follow. Ron and I made a mad dive into a butcher's shop and under his chopping block. The place shook and there were pieces of shrapnel landing all round in the road outside, which we found to be very hot when we went and tried to pick them up."

Dorothy Gray of Waterford Road, Ipswich, also has vivid memories of the same attack.

"I lived 'over Stoke' at the time but worked as a receptionist/telephonist at E R & F Turners (Bull Motors), Foxhall Road. It was a murky, misty day and I left work about 4.30pm (we worked shifts) to cycle home round the docks to Stoke. As I left work I was going towards Foxhall Road bridge

Fire drills were obviously vital in ensuring everything was done correctly in the event of an attack. Here, the fire brigade's boat is in action during a training session in Ipswich Dock in 1940.

– suddenly this plane came towards me, very low, firing a machine gun. You could see the flashes from the gun and the 'Swastika' markings. I stopped cycling and froze. An elderly couple nearby threw themselves to the ground near a wall, I thought they had been hit, but they were alright, just shaken."

"As the sound of the bombs had come from the way I was going, I worried about my mother over Stoke. So I continued my journey. When I got to near Salthouse Street, I was stopped as the shop opposite the public house had been hit and I had to go all round the town

to get home. It was a very frightening experience and whenever I go that way the memory always returns."

"How this plane avoided the barrage balloons that were up that day was a tribute to the skill of the German pilot. The sirens went off after the bombs."

"My boyfriend, now my husband, worked for Ransomes and Rapiers over Stoke. He was eighteen-years old, when after another raid, he had to go into work to help clear up those killed in the machine shop after a booby trap bomb (like a tin can) which was dropped on October 27/28 1940. The men were on night shift. A memorial to the men that died that night was erected in Bourne Park."

"Office girls had to do fire watch at their firms. They had to go through smoke-filled rooms and climb down on rope ladders from high buildings as part of their training."

ABOVE This huge fragmentation bomb fell into the swampy ground of Holywells Park, Ipswich 7 January 1941 but failed to explode. It took six days to defuse and clear. The team of Royal Engineers who dug the bomb out are with members of the Ipswich Borough Police Force.

Bombing

Cyril Garnham of Harkstead who takes a keen interest in the local history of World War Two said. "I lived in Harmony Square until 1943 with my parents and two brothers, Peter and Arthur. Enemy aircraft were frequently over the town and broken nights sleep were a feature of daily life. On the night of August 25, 1942 the raiders were met by particularly heavy anti-aircraft fire which almost certainly forced one of the

planes to drop two 500kg high explosive bombs. The first of these fell in the wooded grounds of Derby Lodge, next to the Duke of York public house at the junction of Woodbridge Road and Warwick Road. The bomb failed to explode and was removed from beneath a beech tree by a bomb disposal unit some five days later."

"The second bomb punctured the rear roof of

the nearby Mission Rooms and passed through the building and out through the ground floor window, where it buried itself in the soft earth. At the time, my parents, my brothers and I, together with an elderly neighbour, were bundled together in a Morrison shelter, which occupied nearly the entire front room!"

"After waiting for the debris and dust to settle and on the

LEFT The image was taken on 8th January 1941 when 10 50Kg bombs fell on the Gainsborough Estate. A woman died in this house on Romney Road.

assumption that the bomb had exploded, we ventured out, together with neighbours, to provide any assistance necessary to the occupants of the Mission Rooms."

"To our amazement an elderly couple – a Boer War veteran and a lady who was deaf and dumb, were sleeping downstairs had a miraculous escape and were unhurt. The bomb must have passed immediately over them. Having found out that there was nobody injured, neighbours returned to their homes only to be advised by the police and air raid wardens to evacuate our homes shortly afterwards, we had been standing on an unexploded bomb!"

"We were taken to a large house on Woodbridge Road prior to being transported by bus to Holywells Park mansion, which was used as a rest centre. We stayed the night and the next day

found temporary accommodation with friends. Eventually on August 30 we returned home and I recall watching the defused bomb being rolled away before being taken away in a lorry for disposal. Fortunately the bomb had caused no causalities and limited damage to property – several houses had previously been damaged when the mine exploded in Cemetery Road on September 1940."

"Tragically on the same night as the above incident, a house at the junction of Nacton Road, Lindbergh Road was demolished by a bomb that killed a mother and eight children – such is luck of the draw in wartime!" (see picture page 32)

"The 'square' consisted of two mews of small terraced houses standing opposite each other and separated by thin front gardens and an

ABOVE The unexploded bomb deep in the ground on Holywells Park Ipswich in 1941. This huge bomb did not explode and residents were left almost unscathed by what could have been a massive loss of life.

unmade area, used by children as a play area. At one end of the square stood a large building occupied by Whitfield King Stamp Company which had access from Lacy Street and at the other end and backing on to the houses on Woodbridge Road stood the Mission Rooms – a two-storey building providing accommodation for the elderly. Harmony Square, no longer exists – it was demolished in the late 1950s and is now the site of old people's accommodation, Hanover Court."

The huge docks in the East End were badly hit with massive fires around the area.

The primitive equipment available to the crews of both the full time professionals and the auxiliary teams meant they had to risk life and limb to stop the huge fires.

These local crews had to fight fires in London and other parts of the region too.

Bernard Jasper of Ipswich . Bernard said "my late father, Albert Jasper. He was a 'career' fireman, having joined the local service before the war started. At some point the service became the NFS, so that there was national co-ordination during the war."

"My father told me many a tale when I was a child, of his experiences attending the huge fires during the London Blitz, especially the raid on Purfleet, the oil terminal. He told me that on the way down the A12 they could see the glow from London even before they had reached Chelmsford, and they wondered what they were in for. He spoke of what it was like to be bombed at close quarters, while trying to fight the flames."

Fighting the Fires

Fire fighting during the Second World War called for a special kind of bravery. During the Blitz London was the prime target for German Bombers. Almost every day and night the capital was in danger as thousands of tons of bombs rained down from the sky.

ABOVE The Auxiliary Fire Service water unit based at Cavendish Street, Ipswich during the early 1940s. These brave men encountered huge amounts of danger on an almost daily basis.

Houses in Bixley Road, Ipswich, close to the junction with Felixstowe Road, were badly damaged in the air raid of 2 June 1942. Numbers 123, 125, 127 and 129 were hit by the blast. At 125 four people had a remarkable escape. They were in their Morrison shelter (in the centre of the picture). The shelter was a steel gage used in the home. They were among ten people trapped in the rubble after the raid

"After the war, his interest in fire fighting and fire brigades never waned, and he built up one of the largest collections of international fire brigade memorabilia in the country, and had contact with brigades worldwide. A range of his items is set out at the Princes Street fire station in Ipswich, as the 'Jasper Collection'. Tom Scrivener of Heron Road, Ipswich, worked with the fire fighters as a messenger. Tom said. "I joined the First Service as a messenger on November 16, 1943. I was not old enough to be a full time fireman. We were based in a large house in Oban Street, off Anglesea Road, when on duty we had to sleep there and if we were called on we had to report to a fire station where Bromeswell Road is now, we also did our training there. We had a Aston van and a Coventry Climax pump kept at Gosling's Garage, London Road, near the Ipswich

Arms public house, which is now demolished. In training we had to climb up a tower using a hook ladder."

"I once went with a full time crew to an American Air Force base at Rattlesden near Stowmarket. I have clear memories of a hanger full of sacks of sugar, a rare sight during the war."

John Powell of Ipswich related a story told to him by his father-in-law of the dedication the fire fighters showed. "My late farther-in-law Reginald Thurlow of Thackeray Road Ipswich told me about his time in the Civil Defence Corp during the Second World War.

They were called out to fires in Norwich, when they returned to Ipswich they went straight on to fight fires in London. He said they were on their last legs when they got home to the

ABOVE Eileen Given was the first woman employed by the Ipswich Fire Brigade. She joined the service 1 September 1939 just two days before the outbreak of World War Two. As a whole, women had a huge role in the war effort, they showed bravery and skill to cope with the amazing circumstances in which they found themselves.

ABOVE LEFT The Auxiliary Fire Service crew at Footman's town centre store with their ladder carrying car on Tower Ramparts during World War Two.

Ipswich depot."

The nightmare of air raids and second hand chewing gum is still with Pauline Clark (nee Goldsmith) who now lives in Hamilton, Ohio. U.S.A. Pauline recalled her time in Ipswich. "I used to live at 75 Beechcroft Road Ipswich. "I can still remember the German Planes coming over during World War Two. I still get

The Auxiliary Fire Crew at Cobbold's brewery during World War Two. When they were called into action, the Auxiliary Fire Service proved its bravery time and again.

very scared at night when I hear a low flying plane. I have awoken many a night out of a deep sleep and told my husband "the Germans are coming". I can remember a girl giving me a piece of chewing gum, which an American had given one of the children. I think it had been chewed by several other children because when it was my turn it had little bits of grit in it. I think I got it for two days and had to pass it on!"

"Imported fruit was not available and the first banana I had after the war I thought it had a bone in the middle of it! Where I live now a siren goes off when there is a Tornado warning and I get really sick to my stomach as it reminds me of the war. I was five years old when it ended but I still remember the sound of the bombs dropping and the planes going over."

A group of Air Raid Wardens at W S Cowell's printing works in the centre of Ipswich during World War Two. These Wardens played a vital role in ensuring that when a raid occurred, they were as prepared as possible.

Air Raid Wardens

Fire fighting is a highly skilled and dangerous job we should leave to professionals. Their advice in the event of fire is, "Get out and stay out". During the days of the Second World War the risk of fire from bombing raids meant that almost everybody had to be ready to tackle a major fire. For those of us

born after the war we can imagine the scale of the terror which struck Ipswich when we see the figures. Ipswich suffered 1165 alerts as bombers crossed the East Coast. This put the whole town in fear as sirens warned people to take shelter. There were 55 air raids which dropped bombs on the

town, 225 homes were totally destroyed and 774 severely damaged.

Tom Pulham of Adelaide Road was only a young teenager early in the Second World War and not old enough to officially be on fire watch duty, but like many lads at the time he found himself getting

Air raid wardens (K group) line up on the Rivers Estate, Ipswich in August 1941.

involved and helping out.

Tom explained that sometimes the training exercises were a little too enthusiastic!

"During the second world war all factories and places of employment had fire watchers. These were employees who served in teams when factories and offices were closed, usually during the night. If any air raids took place and incendiary bombs were dropped they had to tackle any blaze at their works. The equipment available was primitive; we had buckets of sand, water and stirrup pump."

"An incident early in 1943 was at the site owned by Ipswich Gas Company at their Tar Works in Wherstead Road. The house, the last on

the left before Bourne Bridge where the manager Mr King and his wife lived, is still there today. The site included derelict half boarded cottages. Since the tar works was a high risk property a motorised pump had been supplied and plenty of water was available from the nearby River Orwell."

"To test the pump the derelict building, the boarding of which had been well covered in tar, was set on fire. There were also some empty barrels which were then partially filled with tar and creosote and placed in the building. The fire was so intense that the pump could not cope with it and the professional fire brigade had to be called out to deal with it. Some of the Ipswich fire engines were

based just past the rail bridge near Rapier Street on land which was known as The Moorings."

"After the fire was extinguished the firemen had "some words" to say to the gas company employees who were left with very red faces – not only caused by the fire! Fortunately the pump never had to be used due to enemy action – much to the relief of the firewatchers and day staff."

"Firewatchers pay for a shift 5.30pm to 10pm was three shillings and six pence (17.5p) 10pm to 8am was five shillings and six pence (27.5p). The 10pm team also got two cheese rolls and a bottle of beer! A shift was usually three people."

The first bombs to hit Ipswich during World War Two came on the night of 22 June 1940. At 12.20 a.m. Heinkle 111 flying at 18,000 feet dropped bombs over the northern part of town. One of the bombs hit this house in Dale Hall Lane killing Mr and Mrs Robert and Stella Anderson and their maid Miss Ruby Crawford.

The First Bomb to Hit Ipswich

A man, his wife and their maid, were killed in their 'bomb proof' shelter, a fortified ground floor living room. I was working and living in Cotswold Avenue which is very close by, all we heard was a tremendous thud and knew nothing more, until looking and next morning and what a shock to see the devastation of the previous night! I've often spoken of it rarely, of course it was sadly just the first of very many more."

Brian Coleman of Mayfield Road, Ipswich added. "It was on my cycle route to Northgate School from Westholme Road and so I passed and re passed it many times. I had a piece of bomb shrapnel for some years after."

"It was said that the occupants were doubly unlucky. Firstly because all the rest of the string of bombs fell in the fields beyond and secondly because the occupants were sheltering under the stairs as was advised and the bomb carved its way under that part of the house."

"When bombs that fell on St Margaret's Green remind me that I was floating on my back in the Broomhill swimming pool at the time and in my ignorance I remember calling to my friends "Look at those things chasing along behind that plane up there!" A whistling sound soon disillusioned them and me as the bombs fell earthwards." (see pic on p22)

"My curiosity about seeing bombsites was corrected when I cycled to Bixley Road to see bomb damage near St Augustine's Church one Saturday morning. It was indeed fascinating to see that the blast had blown away the walls of bungalows and the roofs had fallen

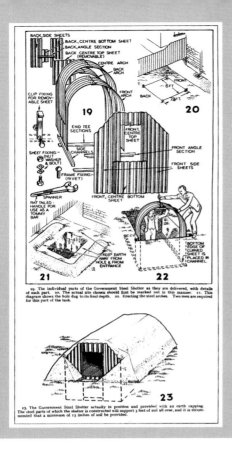

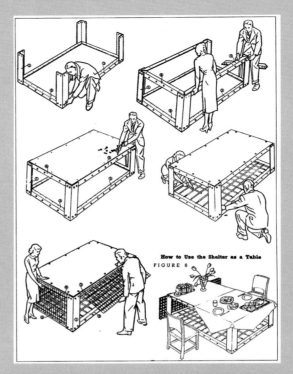

How to Use the Shelter as a Table
FIGURE 8

ABOVE This leaflet showed people how to build their own Anderson air raid shelter. Although these shelters were not hugely effective, they still saved many thousands of lives and gave comfort to all those who had them.

ABOVE RIGHT Morrison Shelters were also very often utilized by residents of Ipswich during the war. This "How to put up your Morrison Shelter" came from a Ministry of Home Security booklet issued in 1941.

down intact. People in a Morrison Table shelter survived almost unhurt."

"Not long after my visit, when I had gone home to dinner, there was an explosion and I found later that the road I had stood on had been blown up by a delayed action bomb!"

When the bomb fell on Myrtle Road my Northgate girlfriend, Beryl Pickess, (in 1946 my wife), who lived nearby, took me to see the dent in the tarmac on Felixstowe Road, where the bomb had bounced. The bomb travelled on clipping the trees in Holywells Park, finally to demolish houses. The bomb was going towards the gas holders at the docks, one of which was of German construction and the low flying 'plane was said to have crashed into a crane on the docks."

War records show that it was June 2, 1942, that Brian

Coleman is referring to. It was just before 2 pm when bombs rained down on Felixstowe Road, Rushmere Road, Bixley Road and Bixley Heath. There were incendiary bombs in Landseer Road, Rivers estate, Sturdee Avenue, Badshah Ave, Shackleton Road, E.R. and F Turners works in Foxhall Road, Dover Road, Exeter Road, Camden Road, Wherstead Road, St Helen's Street, Jefferies Road and Palmeston Road. Five were killed in the raid, including an air raid warden.

ABOVE These houses in Felixstowe Road, Ipswich were hit by a bomb 24 March 1941. Numbers 209 and 211 are opposite Murray Road. Wardens and police rescued five people from the debris.

RIGHT A house in Myrtle Road was destroyed during an air-raid on 2 June 1943.

This house in Woodbridge Road East, Ipswich close to the Rushmere golf course was hit by a bomb 21 September 1940. Mr and Mrs Woodbine were trapped in their Anderson shelter. It perfectly illustrated the type of damage that a bomb could cause.

Houses in Myrtle Road were damaged in an air-raid of 2nd June 1943. Three people were killed and several injured during the raid. One of the German aircraft struck a crane at the dock and near the lock gates

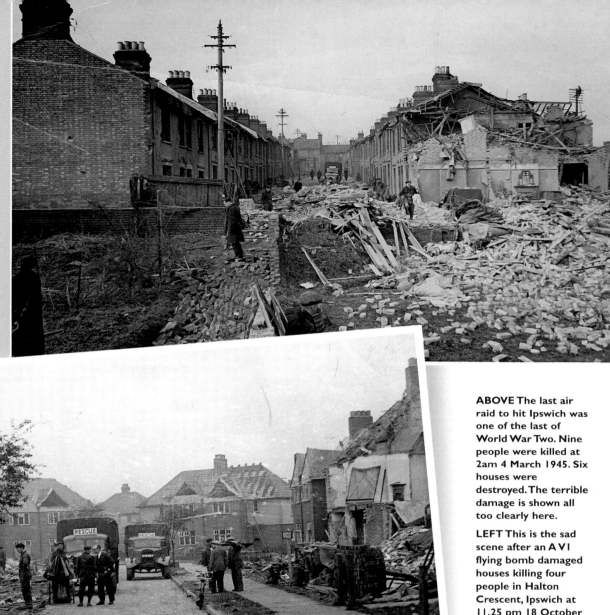

ABOVE The last air raid to hit Ipswich was one of the last of World War Two. Nine people were killed at 2am 4 March 1945. Six houses were destroyed. The terrible damage is shown all too clearly here.

LEFT This is the sad scene after an A V1 flying bomb damaged houses killing four people in Halton Crescent, Ipswich at 11.25 pm 18 October 1944.

Tragedy occurred when a bomb hit an Anderson Shelter in the garden of a house at the junction of Nacton Road and Lindbergh Road, killing 14 people, including a mother and her eight children.

Brian Cobb of Adelaide Road, Ipswich has a story, which shows how propaganda can twist facts during wartime. Brian explains. "Following D-Day a serviceman noticed the name Ipswich on documents belonging to the German news agency. A translation revealed it to detail the

"Destruction of Ipswich on the night of June 2, 1942" as told by a German war correspondent Hans Weiss.

"In graphic terms it records how brave German air crews had run the gauntlet of anti aircraft shells, searchlights, barrage balloons and night fighters, to reduce Ipswich to a smoking heap of ruins. Using experienced bomber crews, who had recently attacked Canterbury as a reprisal for the raids on Cologne and who were said to be conversant with all the tricks of the English air defense, it was believed to have had a 100 per cent success."

"Description of the widespread destruction to the town and its dock installations as characterised by the glow of gigantic fires which were visible for miles, was as we know thankfully greatly exaggerated."

No doubt the German propaganda machine made the very most of the raid, but the reduction of Ipswich to a heap of smoking ruins was of course untrue.

This air raid, which took place on 4 November 1940, struck 132 Bloomfield Street and led to the death of Alan Sporle, a terrible tragedy for the town.

Air-raid Killed Child

Catherine Fosdike of Nelson Road, Ipswich told me of the tragic events of the raid on Bloomfield Street. Catherine said. "It was my parents Arthur and Ethel Sporle who lived at 132 Bloomfield Street, Ipswich when it was bombed on November 4, 1940 at around 11.40am. The raid killed my brother Alan James Sporle, aged only seven years."

"My mother Ethel was heavily pregnant with me at the time, she was very badly injured having been trapped beneath the gas cooker (most probably getting dinner ready), sustaining two broken legs and other injuries. I was born December 16, 1940. My sister Valerie 10 and brother David were slightly injured and were found trapped beneath the wardrobe and ceiling."

"When I think of the trauma my dear mother Ethel suffered. I think her life had been good, having recently moved into a new house, four lovely children, Muriel, Valerie, Alan and David and a new baby on the way. Her husband Arthur had a good job as assistant manager at Ernest Joyce & Co Wholesale Newsagents, Ipswich, all to end that morning, November 4, 1940. My mother, sister and brother suffered very bad nerves for the rest of their lives. I think our house was the only one ever bombed in Bloomfield Street."

American Soldiers

Cookies, chewing gum, silk stockings for the ladies. All sorts of goodies arrived in our area in 1942 when the American forces arrived during World War Two. Airfields sprung up all over the region, there were nineteen in Suffolk. Forces with unfamiliar accents, music, dances and culture started to fill homes and villages. It brought together two very different cultures – young men from the New World and rural communities from the old, most members of both groups having rarely travelled abroad or seen a "foreigner" before.

Every day the sky seemed full of aircraft. Boys dashed to spot aircraft at the new airfields. One of the biggest airfields close to Ipswich was RAF Martlesham. The United States 8th Air Force, 356th Fighter wing arrived, with the 361st, 360th, and 359th Squadrons.

They were originally equipped with P47 Republic "Thunderbolts" - which arrived at Martlesham on 5 October 1943. They were initially tasked to provide fighter escort for B17 and B24 Bombers on their almost daily raids into Germany and the occupied countries of Europe.

In 1944 the pattern changed and they ranged over the Low Countries on low-level missions, attacking U-boat installations, airfields, radar sites, railway depots and sidings.

During November 1944 the Squadrons re-equipped with North American P51 "Mustangs". This aircraft, with its longer range, enabled the Squadrons to revert to long range escort duties for the B17 bombers, on raids deep into Central Europe.

Following the end of hostilities, the airfield returned to being an R.A.F. Station.

There were also other foreign accents heard for the first time by many with Polish pilots and others from occupied countries flying with the RAF. Adding to the mix were German prisoners of war that worked in the area.

Valerie Leathers (nee Thurkettle), of Shetland Close, Ipswich said "I used to live in Spenser Road, Ipswich on the Whitton Estate. I was there from when I was two until I was sixteen when we moved to newly built Chantry Estate. Some of the American Force used to have lodgings in

Byron Road and in Whitton Church Lane, a building was erected which housed a lot of their food rations."

"Several of us children used to go there and we would be given huge cookies on occasions, also we used to say to them "Have you got any gum chum?" The Americans were generous with that."

"There was a concrete water tank erected in Spenser Road. It was used as an extra supply to put fires out. It was very deep and a lad from Whitton Church Lane was trying to retrieve something when he fell in. One of the Allen brothers who lived across the road was alerted (David, I think) and he jumped in and saved his life"

My late father Mr Jack Thurkettle was on fire duty a lot at Reavell's engineering works where he was an engineering blacksmith for forty-three years. My late mum and us five children used to stand under the stairs or under the dining table when the sirens went off. We were terrified as the sky lit up and the doors and windows rattled."

"We were very thankful when we heard the "cuckoo" sound for all clear. We also had an Anderson

Staff at W S Cowell's printing works in the centre of Ipswich prepare for war in the late 1930s. The Buttermarket Shopping Centre is now on this site.

shelter in the back garden which we used at times."

Ted Girling of Maidenhall Approach, Ipswich, has his memories of how the German prisoners worked on the roads in the Whitton area of Ipswich and how tanks were a familiar site on the estate. He also remembers the explosion, which killed one teenager, Harold Osborne, and injured another in 1944."

"I was playing in Keats Crescent a few yards from the explosion. I saw the flash and remember shortly afterwards a boy named Howe running past me with his face covered in blood."

"This tragic event was one of many stressful times experienced by children during those war years. There were also many happy times. Whitton estate played host to the eighth army prior to the desert campaign and we spent many hours with the soldiers."

"Every road on the estate accommodated tanks and other army vehicles. What a playground it was for children in the area."

"Having spent many happy hours with British soldiers we later spent time with German prisoners of war who were transported daily to the fields at the rear of my garden. They worked on the construction of roads around Macaulay and Coleridge Road."

These men, who worked at **WS Cowell's** printing works seem pretty happy with their efforts in constructing an elaborate trench and bunker system which would keep them safe in case of an immanent raid.

The Mobile First Aid team at Heathfields Woodbridge Road, Ipswich in august 1943. They are outside the building used for training in the evenings. It was part of the Poor Law Institution, known as the Workhouse. This is now part of the Ipswich Hospital site. In the front centre is Dr Sidney Scott.

Hospital Memories

Memories of harsh visiting arrangements for children in Ipswich hospital come from Dorothy Casburn of Brunswick Road, Ipswich.

It is hard to imagine such a strict regime for sick children as Mrs Casburn tells us about.

Dorothy said. "When I was seven years old I was in Moseley ward having an operation to remove my adenoids. I was hoping to be in hospital for just a few days, unfortunately complications developed in my ear. My few days turned into eight weeks!"

"Visiting in those days was restricted to once a month. Christmas was in those eight weeks so I was allowed an extra days visiting. Sometimes my parents would come and look through the window to try and see me."

"Christmas was exciting, all the children had presents and the nurses came round singing carols and the ward was decorated. The nurses were very kind but strict. Matron was always on her rounds making sure beds were correctly aligned, and had precise hospital corners."

"I had another spell at Anglesea Road Hospital in Goodrich Ward when I was fourteen, having my appendix out. After the operation I was not allowed out of bed for a week, and no solid food for three days."

"This spell also coincided with Christmas so officially I was not allowed any Christmas dinner, but Mr Hill the surgeon was in the ward carving the turkey and took pity on me and said "For goodness sake give her some dinner."

Mrs V Dobin of Chesterfield Drive, Ipswich, was a child patient at Anglesea Road Hospital in 1927. She said, "I was there to have my tonsils removed. I recall lying in a row with other patients and returning home the same day. I was there again in 1933, as a result of measles, for an operation performed by Mr McKenzie. I had to visit a ward, which overlooked Berners Street, twice a day for six weeks due to a shortage of beds! Even then it was a ward for adults. I was only twelve!"

When they demolished the Anglesea Road hospital I confess to feeling sad, I am glad they left the main building with the columns at the entrance."

Members of a first aid team at the ambulance station behind the E.U.R public house in Croft Street. The bus in the background had been converted to a first aid post. In the centre of the front row is Dr Burns, the Assistant Medical Officer of Health. Photograph from Gladys Frost (fifth right, front row).

A Bridge too far

Joyce Partridge remembers the day during World War Two, when gliders flew over Ipswich on their way to the "Bridge to Far" battle at Arnham Holland in 1944. Joyce was working as a volunteer in the centre of Ipswich at a canteen and rest rooms for members of the women's services.

Margery Race, of Penryn Road Kesgrave has vivid memories of that day, she was one of the local girls who took over the duties of men working on the Ipswich trolley buses. Margery said. "During the war I was a driver on the local trolley buses. On the day all the gliders were going over Ipswich, I was driving along Norwich Road. My conductor, May Offord, came to the cabin, and was crying, saying her husband was in one of the gliders. We then continued our outward trip, both of us crying all the way, we had the sympathy of many people that day. He survived the landing and was hidden by a Dutch doctor until being captured by the Germans. He spent the rest of the war as a prisoner. He

and the Dutch doctor remained friends for the rest of their lives. Working on the buses we had good times and sad times, the memories linger on."

Nancy Rudd (nee Monk), of Foundation Street, Ipswich, also worked at the canteen recalled by Joyce Partridge and tells us more about the service, which helped to keep spirits high during the grim days of World War Two.

Nancy said "Memories came flooding back after reading the story from Joyce Partridge. I knew her when she was Joyce Rockett and I was the Nancy Monk she mentioned.

The canteen was in two large rooms, a stones throw from the Town Hall, above Adolphus Tears, the photographers in The Walk. On one side our windows looked down onto Tavern Street and the other ones looked down The Walk towards Cornell's and Grosvenor Fashions."

"It was after our supervisor Jean Foyster left us that I took over and subsequently learned about some of the

difficulties our committee had to deal with before even we could boil our first kettle of water to brew our first pot of tea."

"Apparently no way would the Ministry of Food grant licenses to new applicants. Eventually a way round the situation was found with the YWCA coming to our rescue. The solution was, we could sell food and drink and be covered by their licence, if we would include their name in the venture. So the Trefoil (our emblem) and Triangle (YWCA emblem) was born."

"Several of the YWCA ladies did a morning shift at the canteen, three names spring to mind – possibly because they used to take over from me at the end of my shift, a Mrs Armstrong, Mrs Harrison and Mrs Quinton."

"We bought our provisions at the Maypole – a shop no longer with us, it was between Tower Street and Hatton Court so it was near and handy for us. Our bread and cakes were purchased from another "no longer with us" shop, but one that I am sure will be remembered

Women worked on the Ipswich busses during World War Two were involved in many instances of danger and bomb raids. The jobs that they did were vital to the effort as a whole.

by many– the Oriental Café in Westgate Street. A young man, riding a trade bicycle with a very large wicker basket fixed on to the front, delivered our order to us. He was Roy Grimwood; we started school together at St Matthews in 1925 where our teacher was a lovely lady – a Miss Colman. One of the shops opposite to our entrance in The Walk was Dunt's Cream Dairies so we had no problem with obtaining milk."

"It was a grand war effort by all the guiders, cadets, rangers and guides who faithfully turned up to work their shifts seven days a week through those long years of war. I like to think we helped Miss Gibb to achieve her idea, dream if you like, of providing a quiet, homely place where the Land Army girls and those in the

services could come and relax in their off-duty time. They would write letters, read, knit, have forty winks or just have somewhere quiet where they could all recharge their batteries and get away for a few moments, from the hurly-burly of service life."

"I remember that Sunday Joyce speaks of, when our Suffolk sky was filled with aircraft towing gliders, having seen it who could forget? What a magnificent sight, but sobering too, when one gave thought to where those brave lads were heading – and the horror that awaited them on arrival."

Audrey Leckenby (nee Gould) also worked at the canteen. Audrey said "The Trefoil and Triangle canteen to which she refers was

housed over shops in 'The Walk', and opened in the early days of World War Two. Members of the YWCA and Ipswich Cadet Guides, which I was a member of, staffed it out of hours. I served there until 1943 when I joined the WRNS. There are still several of my generation living in Ipswich who served in the canteen."

Mrs J Millyard was twenty-years-old and working in the Woman's Land Army, working the fields just over the border into Norfolk when the aircraft taking part in the D-Day landings of 1945 flew over.

Mrs Millyard said "I joined the Land Army in 1942 and stayed until 1945. On D-Day in 1944 I was working on a field near Harleston with a gang of other girls, when we heard the noise of aircraft overhead. We all stopped working and looked up to the sky and saw hundreds of planes pulling gliders behind them. We shaded our eyes from the sun to get a better view. We all wondered where they were going, not a clue. Eventually we got to know the next morning on the radio; it was the D-Day landings. I will never forget the sight of those planes. I was stationed at Flixton, Norfolk. I still have my WLA armband and my discharge certificate from Mrs Sunderland Taylor, head of the War Agricultural Committee."

Women working for Ransomes Simms and Jefferies during World War II

Industry

Ipswich was an engineering town. Most families had somebody working for one
of the giant employers like Ransomes Sims and Jefferies, Ransomes and Rapier,
Cranes Ltd, Reavell and Company, E R and F Turner Ltd, Bull Motors, and The
Manganese Bronze and Brass Company. At shift change time a hooter, known a
"The Bull" would sound and thousands would fill the streets on foot and cycle

Relatively little is left of the town's engineering history with most of the sites
cleared and replaced by smaller industrial units or housing.

During the war years men were called up into the armed service and woma
took over the jobs traditional done by men. They worked on munitions in
engineering works or operated the town's busses, while others joined the
Women's Land Army to help feed the nation.

Women's War

Winston Churchill said, June 1940, in one of his famous speeches during the Second World War, "We will not flag or fail–we shall go on to the end–we shall fight in France; we shall fight on the seas and oceans. We shall fight with growing confidence and strength in the air. We shall defend our island whatever the cost may be."

Stirring stuff. As the country faced invasion the need for equipment to fight the war on land and sea was top priority.

As men were sent away to fight the war with the armed services this produced a massive labour shortage and woman had to fill the gaps left in the factories.

ABOVE Female staff at Ransomes Sims and Jefferies during World War Two learning how to use a micrometer. This complicated lecture ensured that the job were done properly, after all, there was nothing more vital to the war effort than ensuring good quality armaments.

LEFT Some of the female staff at Ransomes Sims and Jefferies during World War Two. The photograph was taken at the Duke Street, Ipswich works. The company continued with its traditional production of agricultural machinery but also worked on munitions.

All of this came in an era when females traditionally did work in offices etc. They soon proved they could match anybody on the factory floor, keeping production going at a vital time for the country's survival.

Daphne Hughes of Ward Road, Ipswich, was one of the girls working on munitions.

"We were friends during the years I was employed at RS&J, which was from 1940-1944. I was engaged as a Junior Clerk in the office of "E" Department. The office housed three foremen, Mr. A Andrews, Mr. E Rowerth, and Mr. A Horne, the senior of which was Mr. A Andrews."

"I was almost 15-years-old at the time and having recently left school was very naïve. I can recall one or two instances where the Engineers – who came to me to make out their tool order requests, would take advantage of my tender years to play jokes. I fell for the usual request at the tool store which called for a "long weight", and I waited there some time before the penny dropped."

"In those days my uniform for office work consisted of a belted cotton smock over my daywear. I recall one time, when an engineer came into the office and asked me to issue the usual tool order for him. It was some time later; while seated at my desk, having completed my rounds of several offices, that Mr. Horne alerted me to the fact that I was wearing a "bobble

A posed photograph of women filing the corners on Merlin engine gears at Ransomes Sims and Jefferies during World War Two. In the foreground is Daphne Hughes

LEFT This image shows women welding mine sinkers at Ransomes Sims and Jefferies during World War Two. Their clothing would suggest the photograph was a posed publicity picture.

BOTTOM Women are shown here inspecting bomb parts at the Ransomes Sims and Jefferies Orwell works during World War Two. This was a vital job and one which was done with much care by these women.

A group of staff line up for a photograph outside the Phillips and Piper clothes factory in Old Foundry Road, Ipswich in October 1945.

on my back". The bobble consisted of a wire hook hanging from the back of my belt, to which was attached a dangling length of string with attached ball of straw. Was I embarrassed! (I never discovered the culprit)."

"My time in the office ended when I realised how lonely the job could be, and that the girls on the shop floor appeared to be enjoying their work much more – I could hear the occasional singing, talking and laughing whenever I passed by. My boss was aghast when I asked him if I might join them, but realising I was serious he agreed, and it was not long before I found myself working as a 'girl fitter' filing burrs off engine gears, along with two other girls – Peggy Harrall and Doris Shepherd. Peggy, an exceptionally

Women played a vital role in production during the war. As well as munitions, these factories also produced agricultural machinery.

Joan Whitson (second left, back row) taking a lunch break with her friends at Ransomes Sims and Jefferies during World War Two.

pretty girl, met a colleague called Jack Withers, whom she later married. During my time on the shop floor, management was preparing a company booklet for publication, and we three girls were subjects of a photograph included in the book. I was given a copy at the time, and still have it today."

Joan Whitson (nee Munson) of Suffolk Place, Lime Kiln Road, Woodbridge, was one of the workers featured in the group photograph. Joan, who is now nearly eighty years old, has a picture taken at the time with her Kodak Brownie box camera, which she still has! The picture was taken during a lunch break of a group of female workers sitting on a plough.

Joan added, "I spent six years at Ransomes Sims and Jefferies. As the buses were not very reliable I used to cycle from Melton every

day. Luckily the traffic was not like it is today!"

"I still have the tapes we wore on our jackets. Red letters on navy blue W.I.V.S (Womans Industrial Nation Services) and my workers pass."

Buses During the War

Recollecting the group of female staff who kept the buses running in Ipswich during World War Two. Joan Read of Allenby Road, Ipswich said, "They nicknamed me 'Buddha' because I had a lucky charm of one on my lapel. We used to have our break in the Public Hall in Westgate Street. We played darts and enjoyed a toasted bun from Newsteads; they were big and tasty. I think the toasted bun was 2d, in old money."

"I enjoyed every moment I was a "clippie", even though we had air raids to contend with. We used to help the elderly on and off the bus, also children used to give up their seat to the elderly, not like now, they still sit while elderly with walking sticks stand. My, how things have changed."

"My late husband Stanley also worked on the buses. He was known as 'Stan the Man' because he was always telling jokes. Mrs G Roper of Rushmere Road, Ipswich,

also worked on the Ipswich trolley buses during World War Two. Mrs Roper said, "I worked for three years as a conductress."

"On one trip to Whitton I was really frightened. When the bus was near the Whitton Maypole public house the bombs were dropping."

"My driver had left the bus and I was alone, I lay down inside the Maypole floor until the raid was over. As I was alone with the bus I decided it was better to start walking back to the Cornhill, the driver of a big tanker offered me a lift. He wasn't quite sure of the way and started to go round by Lister Road which had been bombed. He took me as far as the Electric House, I was so grateful I gave him a half crown out of my own pocket. I walked to the Cornhill. It was now very foggy and there was a bus running to the depot, the driver wanted someone to walk in front, as his

conductress was afraid I did, although I just wanted to get to the depot and then to my home. I had to walk home from Constantine Road to Belvedere Road."

The raid Mrs Roper recalls is possibly that of November 3 1943. German bombers JU 88's dropped bombs in the Dales Road area cutting the railway line. Four bombs landed in Norwich Road, two on Brooksfield Road, one in Kitchener Road, Bramford Road, All Saints Road, Yarmouth Road, Gatacre Road, the Greyhound Track in London Road. Fire pots landed in Spencer Road, Raeburn Road, and Hogarth Road. Incendiary bombs landed in Rushmere Road, Mill Farm Westerfield, Dale Hall Farm, Castle Hill, Bramford Lane allotments, Brockley Crescent, Ashcroft Road, Western Senior School (now Westbourne High). Three people died in the raid.

Women at War

plate was for when I was about eight years old).

My aunt had and kept Victorian values throughout her 90 years of life, but like thousands of others was thrown into a very different world as men were taken away to fight the Second World War. Part time work became compulsory for woman of 18 to 45.

No doubt women were just as capable of welding, riveting, driving huge machines and working in the foundry as the men. Traditionally though it was the men who took on the hard manual work.

September 1939 saw the start of the Second World War. It was the year Ransomes Sims and Jefferies celebrated their 150th anniversary at Ipswich. The Orwell Works made 17 pounder gun carriages, components for the Merlin Engine used for Spitfire and

As I grew up in Ipswich in the 1950s I always found it difficult to imagine my genteel maiden aunt as a welder, making tanks and the like at Ransomes Sims and Jefferies during the war.

My aunt, who would sit in her home knitting quietly in the corner when I visited her, was the kind of lady who would serve me a bag of crisps on a plate (great confusion as to what the

At Bredfield the local blacksmith did more skilled work. The village groups completed over 80,000 hours of work.

Much of the normal work of the company continued as agriculture equipment was also vital to the war effort of food production.

It was October 1945 before R, S, and J produced the last horse drawn plough. The last Motrac plough, the 30,000th, rolled of the production line. It was a major achievement to keep production going during the war as there were constant problems finding components and people power.

The war effort owed a great deal to "Girl Power" and all the ladies who swapped their dresses for overalls and got stuck into the jobs of the factory floor.

Hurricane fighter aircraft, and bomb trolleys, parts for Crusader tanks and other items for the war effort.

One amazing piece of equipment was like a plough built on the front of Churchill tanks.

The plough units cleared a path for the tank tracks through mine fields. Two hundred mine-clearing devices for tanks were made in the months up to D-Day.

Many of the women worked in units at outlying villages who were unable to get the factory near the dock. Ladies of the parishes were supplied with benches and tools so they could work in their own homes and sheds.

Jobs included salvaging, sorting re threading nuts and bolts and assembling plough wheels. The ladies of Playford did fitting and de-burring work in their own homes, while at Waldringfield they made parts for the Motrac plough.

The crew of a steam shunting engine at Ipswich dock around 1930. The railway provided a vital link in the passage of good from one town to another.

Days of Steam

"There is a train crossing the A12 at Capel St Mary" This is a statement which would stop any motorist in his tracks. Until the Hadleigh branch line was closed in 1965 there was a crossing point for the line over the main Ipswich to London

Road at Capel St Mary.

Barbara Brown of Beechcroft Road, Ipswich, worked for the line and remembers some of the goods carried by the service. "In July 1940 I started my career on the old London and North Eastern Railway

at Hadleigh Station. There were two trains a day, one arriving in Hadleigh at 08.50 and another at around 14.30 hours, both trains staying around one and a half hours to allow for unloading wagons and shunting."

"Joe Marriott was my first station master, he lived in the High Street, and his wife was Registrar of Births, Marriages and Deaths."

"The traffic at the station was quite extraordinary for a place of that size. Regular consignments of day old chicks were despatched by Eastman Bros. of Hadleigh, also shrubs and trees from S J Letts & Sons of Semer. Wilsons Corn & Milling Co despatched each day a wagon of flour to London's Smithfield Market. During the fruit season tons of apples were collected by our lorry from Cook & Sons, French Farm and from Thomas, Town House Fruit farm, mainly to markets in Newcastle and Glasgow. Our lorry driver was Charles Barber, who was an excellent man. The other staff were Mr Powell Spooner (clerk),

Ron Double (checker) Jim Crisp and Herbert Beckett (both shunters)."

"I remember cattle coming in and going out from the station. Every morning the fish merchants G Sisson, Mr Smith, Mr Gregory and Mr Mulberry used to come and meet the first train with their trolleys for their fish coming from Grimsby and Lowestoft. Bob Squirrell, who was a carrier from Bildeston, made daily calls to collect and deliver goods to the country areas."

"American servicemen came to the station to unload train loads of hardcore etc for the runways at Raydon Wood and Hitcham during World War Two. I can recall bombs being dropped on a house at Toppesfield Mill, killing Mrs Halls. The remainder of her family survived, her daughter Bertha married a soldier who manned the ack ack gun in the field where their house was."

"I think the highlight of my experience was my last station master, Ron Calver, who lived in Hadleigh. He had a son called Clive. Often I used to babysit for him. Through a quirk of fate a few years back I discovered that he was director general of the Evangelical Alliance, he now is President of World Relief and works from Baltimore USA. I am very pleased to have made contact with him and we regularly keep in touch."

Audrey Bennett, of George Street, Hadleigh also remembers the air raid of the Second World War. Audrey who then lived in Benton Street said.

"I remember being taken to meet an auntie off the train, when I was about three or four. It was at the station I saw the first slot machine, she gave me a penny to put in the slot, and out came a bar of Nestles chocolate, wrapped in silver paper, with a red paper cover outside, all for one penny."

"Bombs fell near Hadleigh Station during World War Two. They missed the station; some fell, on the nearby allotments, which is now Clopton Garden. One unexploded bomb had to be detonated. Others went in the river by the Mill. The last one hit the Mill House, killing Mrs Halls. She was the only person to be killed in Hadleigh during the war."

When I was ten years old we used to watch the trains arrive and depart with about three or four passengers, towards the end of its days as a passenger service."

"As a child I was taken along the line on Good Fridays because the trains didn't run. We used to go up as far as Hunters Bridge, gathering primroses."

"I worked for the Newth's, who lived at the Flying Chariot opposite the Kings Arms in Benton Street. I

took the children to the station, which by this time was a goods station only, to meet the train to collect a goat. It was too strong for me; it broke loose and bolted, going in a back door in Benton Street, through the house and out of the front door. It was caught later at The Kennels, Layham."

Rosemary Farrow of Felixstowe Road, Ipswich lived in Great Wenham as a child. Rosemary said. "My Uncle Harry Howes who lived near Bentley station worked on the line. He and my father often enjoyed a pint in the Railway Tavern. I remember the trains (goods) and the crossings and the people who lived there. There was a crossing between Little Wenham Church and Park House Farm and further along a crossing behind Jermyn's farm. The Barford's lived there; Miss Barford was a dressmaker and her brother Fred worked on the land. Eventually they lived in Capel Street, at the crossing near the church there was a big family of men the Pittocks. We used to go up to Bottle Bridge and pick primroses and to the other crossings for cowslips."

Women's Land Army girls who were billeted at Hope House, Ipswich looking happy in their work, including Joy Bere (second left front row).

The Land Army

It's me! The call to identify the photographs of the Land Army girls. Pat Coppen of Woodbridge Road, Ipswich answered my appeal to identify the photographs taken in the 1940s of smiling girls.

Pat told me the pictures were taken after the end of the Second World War when she was based at Hope House at the corner of Foxhall Road and Alan Road, Ipswich. The building was used as accommodation

for local Land Army Girls. Pat (nee Bowles) has many memories of Hope House; she was placed there when it was an orphanage. Pat was born in Colchester in 1928 and arrived at the orphanage when she was just eighteen

FAR LEFT, TOP Ipswich based members of the Women's Land Army take a break during harvest time in 1948. The Land Army allowed many women to do their bit for the war effort. The results they achieved were vitally important. Without their help, Britain could not have had the food it so needed.

FAR LEFT, BOTTOM Members of the Women's Land Army take a break with farm workers at harvest time in the 1940s. It was hard work and here some workers are enjoying a well earned break.

LEFT Ipswich based Members of the Women's Land Army enjoying harvest time fun during World War Two. This image seems like a precursor to all those calendars that have followed.

ABOVE A group of Woman's Land Army members who were based at Hope House, Ipswich during World War Two.

Woman's Land Army girls in the grounds of Hope House in Foxhall Road, Ipswich with "displaced persons" who helped with the work. Pat Coppen is seated at the front.

months old. Residents of the home were evacuated to Northampton in 1939. When she returned to Ipswich in 1946 Pat stayed with friends and worked at Churchmans cigarette factory in Porman Road. Soon it was back to Hope House when Pat joined the Land Army where she stayed until she married in 1949.

Pat recalled the way she was taught to milk a cow. "It was hilarious, during the six months training we practised on a bag with water in it!"

Joy Bere (nee Morphew) of Dawnbrook Close, Ipswich

who added "How surprised I was to see myself and my sister-in-law Rose. What happy days they were. I knew most of the girls in the big group photograph at Hope House. We used to go from there, in a lorry or bus, to farms all around Ipswich to work on the land. We used to harvest sugarbeet; it was icy cold in the winter.

We did hedging, muck spreading and many other jobs. It was hard work and we were always glad to get a hot bath back at the hostel".

"We were a happy crowd, always singing on the bus and in the fields. They were the happiest of my working days. An amusing thing was during the war years there were no bananas available to

WOMEN'S LAND ARMY MINIMUM WAGES TABLE.
EAST SUFFOLK.

In operation from December 12th, 1943.

Length of County Week	Age Group	Minimum gross wage	Minimum Net Cash Wage for volunteers employed on the basis of the County Week and BILLETED BY THEIR EMPLOYERS exclusive of overtime	Overtime Rates per Hour	
				Weekdays	Sundays and agreed half days
48 hours winter (8½ on 5 days, 5½ on ½ day) 50 hrs. summer (9 on 5 days. 5 on ½ day)	18 and over	48/-	27/-	1/2d.	1/5d.
	17 - 18	41/-	22/6	1/-	1/2½d.

NOTES.

1. VOLUNTEERS NOT BILLETED BY THEIR EMPLOYERS.
Volunteers not billeted by their employers must be paid a gross wage sufficient to leave them with the Land Army Minimum Cash Wage (22/6 for workers of 18 or over, or 18/- for workers under 18) on a working week of up to 48 hours in winter or 50 hours in summer AFTER PAYING FOR THE COST OF THEIR BOARD AND LODGING. This also applies during the first two months of employment when the weekly wage for inexperienced women agricultural workers is subject to abatement.

2. OVERTIME.
For your guidance we quote the definition of overtime given the Order issued by the

ABOVE A parade of the Woman's Land Army crossing the junction of Crown Street and High Street in the 1940s. All of the buildings featured have since been demolished and the road widened. On the left is the Crown and Sceptre public House, which was demolished in 1961.

LEFT This image shows a Woman's Land Army minimum wage table from World War Two. The sums are hardly much by today's standards, but they ensured a decent living for those hardy enough to take up the challenge.

Joy Bere, front left, with the Women's Land Army near Ipswich, around 1947

pack for our lunch. Those who made our lunch used to boil parsnips and flavour it with banana essence, you could not tell the difference!"

By March 1940, agriculture in England and Wales had lost over thirty thousand men to the armed services. Another 15,000 had left the land to join other occupations. The main reason for this was the low wages paid to agricultural labourers.

During the First World War the government established the Woman's Land Army. The severe shortage of labour persuaded the government to reform the organisation and by 1944 there were 80,000 women volunteers working on the land. The majority already lived in the countryside, but around a third came from Britain's industrial cities.

Women in the Land Army wore green jerseys, brown breeches and brown felt hats.

They did a variety of jobs and a quarter were involved in milking and general farmwork. Others cut down trees, worked in sawmills and over a thousand women were employed as rat-catchers.

This great image encapsulates the reality of holidays in Felixstowe during the period

Leisure

A couple of generations ago holidays were usually spent locally. Few families could afford much more that day trips to Felixstowe to enjoy the coast. A special treat would be a beach hut where the family could base itself after arriving at the resort by train. Until the 1960s the trains from Ipswich would be packed with parents and exited children on warm summer's days. Families boarded at either the main Ipswich Station or Westerfield and Derby Road Stations and then rode to Felixstowe. Very few families had the luxury of their own car.

Most of the larger companies then had active sports and social clubs with football and cricket teams taking part in local leagues.

Raymond Dodman's father Martin on a day out at Felixstowe in 1931. He is on the beach at the bottom of Bent Hill enjoying a bottle of stout and a bag of shrimps. Martin Dodman was a hide and skin merchant working closely with Ipswich butchers and the cattle market. Mr Dodman had a large moustache waxed with a special French cream purchased from a local barber's shop.

Holidays in Felixstowe

Excitement for me as a child in the 1950s came knowing my family was planning a day trip to Felixstowe by train. We would walk with all the goodies for a day out to stand on the platform at Derby Road station, Ipswich, having walked from our home in Cliff Lane, and wait with hundreds of others in the summer sunshine for the train to take us to Felixstowe. At the town station the steam locomotive would change ends to pull the carriages to Beach Station. Colin Campbell, of Chilton Road, Ipswich, was doing the same journey in the 1930s when the train travelled on to the pier at the dock. He has vivid memories of those simple pleasures and watching the activities of RAF Felixstowe. Colin's memories of the 1930s are a delight.

"My family walked from the Colchester Road to Derby Road Station. I was seven in 1933; even now it still seems a long way! It was four and a half pence (about two pence in decimal coins) cheap day return to the Beach Station or five pence to the Old Pier where the Port of Felixstowe is today. Beer was four pence a pint or less. We collected our tickets from the ticket office, and waited with hundreds of others on a crowded platform. First we heard the bell ring in the signal box and Station Masters Office. The Porters then got ready anything to go into the guards' van. If this was an "Old Pier Train", there were plenty of empty shrimp baskets."

"The train whistle sounded as it approached Foxhall Road bridge, and seconds after the puffs of smoke, grinding of brakes, and the whistles of steam and the yells of porters "stand well back please" as the train, already full of day trippers, came grinding to a halt. We watched for the magical ring with a purse, taken to the signal box. Without this the train could not go."

"Sometimes we would wait for the next train; "It's only another quarter of an hour. It'll take us directly to the Old Pier and it'll be empty". It often was. The Old Pier I refer to was the little LNER Pier close to Felixstowe Dock, in between the Dock Pier and the RAF Station at Landguard, where the Flying Boats were. It cost two pence, all day for a fishing ticket. "Come and go as you like. Don't lose your ticket."

"The pier was like an extension to the station. Opposite the entrance, with a waiting room. It was built by the railway company for the river paddleboats from Ipswich, and Shotley. In the 1930s it was used for the Harwich fleet of shrimpers, to discharge their cooked catch in wicker baskets for distribution by the London North Eastern Railway direct to all stations on the line to Liverpool Street (there were 10 stops to Colchester). The "New Pier" on the sea front was the second longest pier in England, second only to Southend on Sea. It had the tram which took us to the Landing Stage a mile off land to meet my Uncle Don who was a Purser on the

"Royal Eagle" Steam Paddle Vessel from Greenwich."

"I enjoyed fishing from the pier, sometimes my brothers dug bait from Nacton Shores the night before a fishing trip. Not so good as the cooked shrimp bait which was perfect for the old pier and useless on the front for the "New Pier.""

"We used hand lines. My father had a rod with an open reel, a three bar paternoster and lead weight. I favoured the hole just above the landing stage where there was a bend in the pier. I always caught a big eel there. In the hot sunny weather we float fished for garfish. A lovely flavour when eaten, not unlike flying fish. Very boney, and an unappetising greenish blue coloured flesh, but you got used to it."

"Silver eels and Flounders were the bulk of our catch, but off this pier I saw nearly every type of fish that lives in the North Sea caught at one time or another. At low tide we scavenged the beach for lost weights, and extra bait. We were warned not to eat the cockles, muscles, clams and winkles that abounded, as these could be polluted. Tube worms and mud rag were plentiful, but if you wanted good lug, you had to walk round the dock, and past the Dooley fort."

"Late evening, before the last train, the strains of various jazz tunes could be heard,

played on a wind-up gramophone by a local jazz club at the local railway hotel. This became the Little Ships pub."

"If we got fed up with fishing. We sat and watched the flying boats at RAF Felixstowe, especially if the Titan crane was in operation (I was working for Kier Ltd when this was blown up to make way for the first Paceco Crane Terminal. The bass killed by the explosion were very nice). We saw the Mercury-Mayor composite aircraft, the Supermarine Snyder Trophy plane, the forerunner of the Spitfire. The new huge Sunderland Flying Boats, so important in the war of the Atlantic and the North Sea Coastal Command. All the Flying Boats and Sea Planes were tested there."

"My first trip to the sea front and promenade was a Sunday school outing. We stopped near the Yacht Pond, and embarked with hampers from the Blue Bird coach. There were wonderful big yachts sailing. These could be hired by the hour or day from a house opposite. We couldn't go near, "In case you fall in". I soon found we were restricted on playing on the sand and not to go near any water. With an Aunt from London, my second visit to the front was much better. "Any more for the motor boat? "Round the bay or to the Lightship

A typical days fun in Felsixstowe for members of the Bean family. People of all ages were able to enjoy the fun on offer at Felixstowe.

Madam? "One and a half to the lightship please." A trip I dreamt of. To go close to the lightship, the wonderful Cork that could be seen in the distance, swinging with the tide. Felixstowe was soon a distant town, and the lightship could be seen clearly. It was red with Cork in great white letters on the side of the hull. Then came a surprise: "We've been given permission to board. Anyone who wants to see how lightship men live, now is your chance." I wasn't too struck with the lack of space, and below decks I felt a bit queasy. It would be a lighthouse for me! The men were very pleased to see us."

"Back on shore there was a fishing competition on the Pier for children. Anything caught alive will count. So crabs were going to play a big part. We nearly all had hand lines with one, two or three hooks. After some four hours fishing I caught a hermit crab in a winkle shell, and a whelk. I came about 200th! The young lady fishing next to me, who put her line in with the start whistle, and played with her dolls, until the finish whistle, pulled out a large flounder, and won the competition. My prize was a combat set. The last prize didn't register a weight. It was a shrimp!"

"For a few years there was an open air swimming pool at Manor House, with a water splash. With calm seas, and warm summer water, the sea creatures could be watched on the sand bar at Manor End, not 20 metres from the shore."

"Some year's mother rented a beach hut for a week or two. We could then have freshly made sandwiches in comfort, and watch the Train Ferry and the Butter Boat from Harwich to the Hook of Holland or Flushing. They left Harwich Harbour and crossed the front of Felixstowe. On a still day, the bow waves were like mountains, even though they were formed some miles off shore."

"One year we were smothered with flying ants, another with ladybirds and once I was caught in a massive flock of butterflies, mainly Peacocks and Red Admirals. Greenfly were also a pest, but none lasting long."

"Sometimes we visited Butlin's amusement park, but with little money to spend we were restricted to a weekly ride on the "switch back". A blue painted wooden construction guaranteed to produce the shriekiest yells."

"Peter's Ice Cream, made in Ipswich, was always on sale somewhere. Sometimes with mother we would visit Bonnies for coffee and petit fours, or afternoon tea at Millers with strawberries and cream cakes."

Broom Hill Swimming Pool

Memories of Broom Hill Pool include family picnics, swimming galas, school swimming lessons and more.

Ray Harvey, of Westholme Road, Ipswich, recalls those school trips when it always seemed to be freezing cold.

"It was early one May morning in 1955. It was cold. I was one of about 30 Westbourne schoolboys standing on the edge of the pool in just our swimming trunks, shivering.

Our master kept shouting at us, "Get in, it's not cold. " He was wearing a hat, scarf and overcoat!"

Ray Riches of Shafto Road, Ipswich, takes us back to the early years.

"I was only six months old, when just before Christmas 1936 my parents moved into Kensington Road, Ipswich, just round the corner from Broomhill Pool. It had just started being built.

"The war had been on for a year, 1940, when my brother aged eight who suffered from severe asthma was medically advised to learn to swim to stretch and strengthen his lungs."

"Two of the attendants of Broomhill Pool, were experienced swimming instructors, too old to fight a war. So at the age of four I started paddling and imitating my brother in the small pool, while he had his lessons in the big pool."

"When aged seven, we moved up to Springfield Junior School in 1943, and were told we all had to learn to swim. Remember there was a war on, rationing, blackouts and winters were long and freezing cold and summers were very hot and went on for months."

"Our first lesson in 1944 started at the end of April, still so cold, we arrived at the pool at 9am still wearing overcoat, scarves and gloves. Talk about breaking the ice!"

"After lessons, because some kids were so slow to redress again (needed teachers help), instead of lining us up in the cold to march in file back to school, we were sent off as soon as we were ready. My best friend Dave Norris and I were first off and called in home on route. Mum had ready hot cocoa or Oxo, and

toast and dripping, (biscuits were on ration)."

"We did this for several weeks until the temperature rose. No one at school ever knew we did this."

"During the war everything was in short supply, especially money. It was normally 3d child and 6d adult. The pool opened at 8am daily, and after the war closed about 9.30pm during July/August/September."

It was only 2d before 9am, so we arrived about 8.50am in the summer of 1946/48 and went home for dinner at 12.30pm."

"They also sold books of 12 tickets for 2/- (i.e. 2d each), save a penny again for two bread rolls at half a penny each. So at 2pm we went back to the pool with our tickets, rolls, sandwiches etc."

"Mums and some dads came up some evenings about 7.30 and we all stayed till closing, as there were lights to illuminate the pool underwater."

"Also about 1946/47, scaffolding was erected on top of the 15 metre board to 30 metre high for an exhibition of high diving."

Sadly mum died in 1948 (Dad didn't come back from the war) and I had to move to the other end of town, near to Pipers Vale Pool, not half as good as Broomhill Pool."

Jack Potter of Bennett Road,

ABOVE Bathing beauties enjoying the Broom Hill swimming pool.

Ipswich wrote with his memories. " In the late 1940's and early 1950's I spent many happy days at Broomhill Swimming Pool. The admission price was about six old pence and before 8am two old pence. The pool closed for an hour at lunchtime but stayed open until 8.30pm or early dusk."

"I learnt to swim at Broomhill and was able to jump off the top diving board when I was six-years-old and if Mum and Dad came to watch on a Sunday afternoon this earned me an ice-cream wafer or a cup of hot Bovril."

"I attended Springfield Junior and Westbourne Secondary Modern schools and they held their annual swimming galas at the pool, as did other schools."

" There were also many of the senior swimming clubs who would hold their galas on Saturday evenings, for these as well as the spectators, seats would be arranged on the swimmers relax area."

"In the late 1940s swimming entertainment troops would display their skills with the top board being built up to double its height and a pair called Marco and Polo would perform fantastic stunts from the extended top board."

" There was also a Tarzan who would fall from the top board after being supposedly shot by the white hunter who would then swim one and half-lengths underwater. Also included were Ester Williams type swimming girls and a man who would do a log roll with half a tree. All very entertaining and exciting stuff for us kids."

"In about 1948-49 glamour girls' show, who were performing at the Hippodrome Theatre. Billed as "Jane" which we were told was based on the comic strip Jane of the Daily Mirror, spent an afternoon at the pool much to the pleasure of us 14-15 year olds, who sat in awe as they changed costumes on the bathers leisure side."

"It was quite a regular trip for my family in the late 1960s early 1970s to go for an early morning swim on Sundays, followed by a good breakfast on returning home, and I know many other families also did the same."

"I still think of it as the best pool in the area and have many happy memories."

The Hippodrome

Music Hall days in Ipswich were recalled when I featured the Hippodrome Theatre in St Nicholas Street, Ipswich. The days of jugglers, singers and comedians brought memories flooding back.

Ken Bean of Dales Road, Ipswich, who is best remembered by thousands for his time as proprietor of the First Floor Club when it was the nightspot in Ipswich, explains how the theatre set him on the path of providing entertainment in the Ipswich town centre.

Ken explains how his family provided lodging at their High Street, Ipswich home to many who were to become household names.

"My fondest recollections were in the 40s during and after the war, when many stage artists from the Hippodrome stayed the week at our family house at 48 High Street, Ipswich, so some of our meal times were particularly interesting."

"Among them were the whole Henderson family, Dick and his wife, the singing girl Henderson Twins and their brother Dickie Henderson Jnr who became a television star in the 1950s and 60s". Other names from our family diary of the 1940s were Randolph Sutton, The Two Leslie's, Frankie Howard, band leader Felix Mason, Old Mother Riley (Arthur Lucas and Kitty Mc Shane).

"My mother's sister Vera Webb also provided "digs" for Hippodrome artists at her home in Foundation Street."

"I remember vividly the singer Dorothy Squires and her younger husband Roger Moore, then a song and dance man in the show, before he was elevated to action films and ultimately James Bond". Dorothy stayed at our home with her first husband, who was, I think Billy Read the composer. They were incidentally the only people to be asked to leave for unruly and noisy conduct."

"As a result of these connections we were often given complimentary tickets to the Hippodrome Shows including the Daily Mirror's

A group of Ipswich Town Football Club players enjoyed a night at the Hippodrome in the 1930s.

The Hippodrome building during its glory years. Throughout the 1930s and 40s, it was a place where people could put the horrors of war to the back of their minds and watch some of the finest acts around.

Jane with her striptease act, very different from today's shows as she was not allowed to move when the curtains were opened!"

"My brother Ted became the Spotlight Operator at the Hippodrome and then joined the Army. Sister Joyce became a Land Army Girl and my youngest brother Ray went in the Royal Navy, while I opted for the Royal Air Force."

"Strangely, I maintained a connection with the old Hippodrome when it became a ballroom and Top Rank Bingo Hall, being invited to become their first Bingo Caller and Head Waiter for the intervening banquets."

"The Mervyn Dale Band with lead singer Harry Kitchen provided the interval music during the bingo, and as soon as I took stage to call the numbers they quickly adjourned to the Oxborrows public house in St Peters Street for refreshments."

"On one occasion I could not start as someone had stolen a bingo ball (No 34 ironically my age at that time) and with no management staff present, I had to appeal for someone to fetch another Ping-Pong ball from their home or anywhere to be able to continue. As this took about 20 minutes, I was alone on stage and decided for the first time ever to try stand-up comedy."

"I resorted to telling jokes that I knew from another Hippodrome regular – Max Miller, but being careful not to repeat the joke that had him banned from the BBC! My starting fee then was a massive £2 per session and I stayed there for two years until Top Rank decided to go full time, which clashed with my own expanding bingo empire in Felixstowe, Leiston, Harwich, Bury St Edmunds and Ipswich. Happy days! This was my beginning of a career in night clubs."

Mr F Symonds of Derwent Road, Ipswich remembers that the theatre was not the warmest place during the severe winter of 1947.

"One memory was of that very cold winter of 1947 and I was there watching the second house performance. The artist on stage was a cabaret star, Kay Francis, who sang songs whilst accompanying herself on the piano. After the first song, she stood up, and asked the audience if they would mind if she put on her fur coat, this she did and carried on till the end of the show."

"Another artist who was a regular visitor was Big Bill Campbell, who with his band played Country and Western."

In the 1930s the Hippodrome was a cinema, the price to get in was four old pence, and I went there quite regularly.

Michael Quinn, of Wellesley Road, Ipswich visited the theatre with his family.

"Mum and dad would take my two sisters and myself to the Hippodrome most weeks in the 50s, which we found most enjoyable."

"I remember singers Malcolm Vaughn and Kenneth Earle, Ronnie Hilton and Big Bill Campbell & Co, Country & Western singers from the States. I think Big Bill died in Ipswich while appearing here at the Hippodrome, he used to stay at a house in High Street."

"There were the comics, Jimmy James, Gladys Morgan & Co and I believe Harry Worth."

"I seem to remember a circus one time. I just remember elephants on the stage, also an ice show; I often wondered how they managed that. After the show there was plenty of water flowing outside, must have been the ice melting."

"I'm sure mum paid a £1 note for five of us and still got change. There was a sweet shop across the road, very busy before the show, good old days."

G.I. Brides

Daily thoughts of Ipswich, from thousands of miles away, are a feature of life for many whom live abroad and miss the old place. I featured the homesick memories of Pamela Olsen who has been in America since 1969 after marrying an American serviceman who was based at Bentwaters.

Christine Sears (nee Godfrey) tells of her love for Ipswich and Suffolk from across the Atlantic. "I guess I was a GI bride. I always thought that the women that married American Servicemen during World War Two were called GI brides, the rest of us just married Americans."

"I worked at the Airmen's Club at Bentwaters Air Force Base in the cashier's cage. I had heard all the bad things about the girls that went out to the base. I had an aunt that talked me into a job there and I found that it wasn't nearly as bad as I had heard, plus the pay was a lot higher than the Co-op where I had been working on one of the mobile grocery shops."

"I met my husband in November 1968. I had been eyeing him for a number of weeks. When I finally got his attention he didn't stand a chance. I was with some friends at one of the many dances held at the base and we 'just happened' to find ourselves sitting at the table beside him and his friends. He was chatting to one of the girls I was with and they found that they were both from Texas. He asked her out! I couldn't believe it. I'd had my eye on him for ages. Anyway, for one reason or another, they didn't connect and a couple of weeks later when I was working one of the airmen told me his roommate had a crush on me. I asked him to describe his roommate and to my absolute delight it sounded like 'my man'. Sure enough when he arrived at the club he started to talk to me and asked if he could take me home the next night. Not being one to waste time I said " How about tonight?"

"He told me his name was David Glenn and he was from Tyler, Texas. We married at Bethesda Baptist Church in June 1970. In November 1970 we moved to Montgomery, Alabama. I did not like Alabama at all. We moved to Dallas in September 1971 and have been in the Dallas area ever since. My husband died in 1997 but I have two adult children in Dallas so I guess I'll stay here because they are not moving to Ipswich."

"It was December 1986 before I plucked up the nerve to get back on a 'plane and go home. I didn't realise how much Ipswich was home until I got there.

I wanted to stand on the Cornhill and yell " Hey people, I used to live here ...do you remember me? I have missed you more than I ever dreamed I could." I really looked at the people as I walked through town trying to see if I recognised anyone or to see if they might recognise me. I wanted to stop people and tell them how lucky they are to live in Ipswich and how much I envied them."

"I have two sisters here in America. Judy lives in California and Elaine and I share a home in Garland, just outside Dallas. When we go home to Ipswich the three of us meet up and travel together. We all head for the travel stop restaurant on the way from the airport for a cream cake or custard tart, to get our holiday started on the right foot. From there on it's cake shop, fish and chip shop, Woolworth's for Pick 'n' Mix and all the other foods we miss. Sometimes we even have time to visit family in between snacks. I miss my mothers baking. Cheese scones, sausage rolls and the steak and kidney pudding she used to make in the old copper in the kitchen."

"If you mention steak and kidney pudding over here the reaction is 'Yuck, you actually eat kidney?'"

"We usually go home at Christmas. There is nothing quite like Ipswich at Christmas."

"The tree on the Cornhill, decorations in the shops and all the people bustling around trying to get the groceries and gifts. English Christmas cards say Happy Christmas. American cards say Merry Christmas. I like the children's Christmas pageants. You really wouldn't believe some of the things we buy to bring home just because it's British. We all know "British is Best" We have got on the plane home with gallon size jars of Heinz salad cream, cafeteria

size bags of Tetley tea bags, pounds of Cadbury's Roses chocolates and Pick 'n' Mix. I know the customs people in Texas think we're crazy."

"Last time my brother came to visit he bought a dozen custard tarts with him. Lovely!"

"The British have a great travel system. You can get on a bus or train in Ipswich and go anywhere. Upstairs on the front seat of the double decker riding down those narrow country lanes is hysterical."

"I hate that there is a shopping mall in place of Tower Ramparts School. I would love to have been able to go look around all the old classrooms. My other old school buildings are still there, Christchurch School and Smart Street. It used to be such a long walk to school when I was a child, but now I find the distance is not nearly as long as I remembered. Maybe I just enjoy the walk a little more."

"So many of the little things have changed. Conductors on buses, pedestrian only streets, and the currency. The first time I was home and tried to buy something I just held out the money and told the cashier to take what she needed. My sister Denise told her I'd been in jail and didn't know the new money! I still have problems trying to figure it out. When I see something priced at £5.95 I think it's a real

bargain until I realise I'm looking at pounds not dollars. I always end up coming back to Dallas with a purse full of small coins because it's easier to pay with notes."

"I have found so many of the girls I knew in Ipswich are now living over here. Dreena Dinsdale, Cynthia Ness, Sally Sadler, Linda Westley, Carmelita Thompson, Nadine Hoy, and some I have just met through the Finding Friends column of the Evening Star. It really is surprising how many ladies from the Suffolk area are living in America. Lots of us went to the same schools and remember the same teachers and schoolmates. If it wasn't so expensive to get around over here I bet we could have a great reunion somewhere."

"I'm still a British Citizen. Wouldn't change it, I think if God wanted me to be an American Citizen I would have been born over here."

"When I am out of tea bags and getting desperate. I have to go to the British import store in Dallas to get some. I guess you can take the girl out of Ipswich, but thank goodness, you will never be able to take Ipswich out of the girl."

"Most of all I miss my family, my brothers, sisters and their families. I am so envious when they all get together for family occasions and I don't get to go. I have a small Union Jack on my PC at work and my nametag on the desk is a Union Jack with my name on it.

Rule Britannia!"

Susan Hernandez sent me her story from Texas.

"I am a G.I Bride I was born and raised in Ipswich. All of my family, and there is a lot of them, all live in Ipswich. Rushmere, Chantry, Gainsbrough, Whitton, we are all over town. I am married to Salvador Hernandez Jr., he was a Tech Sergeant in the United States Air force, stationed at R.A.F Bentwaters, and we have been married for nearly 23 years."

"When I left Ipswich I was only 21 years old, and thought I knew it all! How wrong I was. When the plane left the ground I cried and cried. When I arrived in Texas, which was my destination, I was still crying. I did not drive a car, did not have fish "n" chips, no neighbourhood pub, no Sunday afternoon cricket matches, no bus to go and come as I liked. The first time I got on a bus over here I got lost. There have been many eventful things, but the most eventful thing that has happened to us is

the Tornado that hit our area called Channelview on Nov 21 1992, this Tornado destroyed thousands of homes including mine! The President of the United States declared it a disaster area."

"The first place I go every time I come home is to Felixstowe, this is my most favorite place in the world! The smell of the onions cooking! The sound of the fountain! The market on Sundays, all of the things I am sure people take for granted who live there. Last, but not least, the fish "n" chips on the corner on the sea front, right outside the arcade, a nice piece of Cod and chips with scraps, there is nothing like it and I can hardly wait, cheers and God bless."

Maureen A. Williams, Winchester, VA feels more at home in the USA although she still loves to visit her other home.

"I too am a GI bride, having left England (and Ipswich) in 1966, pregnant and terrified at the thought that I could be doing the wrong thing and wondering if I would be able to afford the trip back "home" while my Ipswich family were still alive."

"There are so many differences in our way of life here and what we were used to growing up. The things I remember from growing up in Ipswich was knowing how to manage without electricity, TV, TV dinners and many of the modern day conveniences. The reason for this is being "war babies" and as such learned to do without and make our own enjoyment."

"I have been in the US 36 years, have 3 grown sons and 2 grandchildren. I became a widow in 1996 and am a survivor. As much as I love and miss England, and Ipswich, I would not change anything that led me to come to this land. I have embraced this land and the people as mine. This is also my "home".

"This is where my children live and I travel back "home" to England at least once a year, twice when I can manage it.

"My middle son (Michael Williams) is a huge Ipswich Town Soccer fan and a member of their US club. He also travels to his other" home" whenever he can."

Beach Memories

Recollections of the fun of holidays and weekends spent at a Felixstowe beach hut prompted some great memories and photographs from Star readers.

Many remember the days before the Second World War and the effect the war had on the facilities from its outbreak in 1939. Huts were removed and the beach covered with tank traps and barbed wire to defend the country from invasion.

John C Butters, of Claydon said, "Most of the people packing the shore and strolling on the "prom" were "day-trippers" from Ipswich. It was a slightly derogatory term because Felixstowe traders were naturally more eager to serve the guests in hotels and boarding houses."

"But the season for the better off was relatively short whilst the annual invasion from Ipswich could be relied upon from spring to autumn. So we were

tolerated, even though we carried our own nosebags!"

"With Felixstowe only 12 miles away Ipswich was able to use it almost as a suburb. It offered all the facilities of a lido only 9d or 4.5d return away, by train from Derby Road Station. It was also within reach by bicycle along a quiet country road through Nacton, Trimley and Walton and a few athletes walked."

"My recollections of it

began in the early 20s when my parents had a hut on the ground now occupied by Charles Manning's amusement arcade."

"The huts were grouped around a sandy square with the remains of sand dunes where the kids played for hours without fear. A favorite occupation was baking potatoes in little ovens dug into the walls of the sandpits. We learned to swim on the beach opposite, which at weekends was completely filled with Ipswich families not fortunate enough to have huts. They brought with

them all the paraphernalia required for a good day out, shopping bags of food, towels, plimsolls, buckets and spades, kites, beach balls, umbrellas, sunglasses – and those awful cotton swim suits."

"About 1929 or 30 all the huts in our area received notice to quit to make way for Billy Butlin's development, and the Cavendish Hotel. Our hut was moved to a site between the Warden Green and Manor Terrace and we enjoyed its use for nearly 10 years, commuting from Ipswich most weekends from

April to October. We regarded it as part of our home and my father delighted in making it really comfortable with padded bench seats, kitchenette, cupboards, curtains and pictures on the walls. In bad weather it was warm and dry, but mostly we sat outside, or on the beach, and watched the world go by. Folk became more neighbourly at the seaside, co-operating to find lost children and keeping an eye on toddlers in the water."

"Food never tasted better than in sea air after a swim and I shall always remember my mother's sausage dinners, with new potatoes and fresh peas cooked on Valor Perfection oil stove, or fish and chips from Littles shop in Langer Road. Harwich shrimps were bought round in time for tea."

"In my early teens the hut was my base for exploration of Landguard Common, the perimeter of the RAF Station, Felixstowe Dock

A carnival parade along the Felixstowe sea-front around 1930

The Amusement Park in Felixstowe was one of the main attractions that brought the crowds flooding in. An attendant looks on as an unfortunate lady seems to take a nose dive from one of the small boats in the lake!

and Trimly marshes, with which I became more familiar than any part of Ipswich. Watching the train ferries, the butter boats (from Denmark) and the flying boats from Landguard Point was thrilling, especially with binoculars."

"On Sunday evenings my father would take me for a walk along the prom, which was thronged rather like Tavern Street at Christmas. We passed dozens of tea parties in progress in huts on the sea front, and tried not to stare. Father seemed to know many of the people we met. The walks took us through Butlins (quite amazing - a mini Disneyland), along the front past a few of Fenn's bathing machines, the principles of which caused much amusement to the masses who changed under flapping towels on the beach!"

"We listened to the brass band in the Pier Pavilion garden. There were brass jockey scales near the

beautiful pier, nearly a mile long with its own railway train."

"Paddle steamers used the pier for trips round the bay, to Clacton, Margate and even for day outings to Ostend in Belgium (£1, no passport needed)."

"Ipswich lost this exciting venue in 1939 when war was declared and Felixstowe became out of bounds for the duration. Its front became a barbed wire entanglement between concrete blocks. Many of the huts were hastily dismantled that autumn and taken to Ipswich for storage, some becoming superior garden sheds."

"After the war the magic pleasure land of Felixstowe was never recaptured, and Ipswich lost a unique asset it had enjoyed for decades. The motor car had opened up the whole of East Anglia and beyond, so day tripping and foreign holidays became within the means of a more affluent society. Within half a century, Felixstowe changed from an Edwardian resort and military base to a quiet coastal town with its name known worldwide - but as a premier port."

Mrs. D W Philips, of Pimpernel Road, Ipswich added, "When I first met my late husband we had a hut where the market stands at Felixstowe. We had to move off as the Hotel Cavendish was to be built, so moved to

inside the railings in front of the wireless tower, but when war broke out we had to move it out."

"After the war we had a hut on the Wireless Green where we met up with three other families. We all went down to the beach and the children played with old rubber tyres, also we all joined in playing with beach balls. After tea we rounded off those magical days playing rounders".

Mrs. Elsie M Johnson, of Sprites End, Trimley St Mary wrote, "After reading the article in the Evening Star I became very interested so I looked up my possessions of bygone days and have found some which go back to before Second World War."

"It started off in 1936/37; my parents had taken the family to Felixstowe from Ipswich, where we lived then. I had two sisters and one brother, who were much younger than I; they had hired a beach hut for the weekend."

" Walking along the prom in the evening to go to catch a train at Beach Station, we saw a "For Sale" ticket on a hut, mum read it, and said it would be lovely if we could buy it."

"At our hut we were surrounded by parents and all the children, teenagers like ourselves, and made many friends, some for the rest of our lives."

"Our hut was called "Ouseburn" and I would love to know how it got that name,

It stood on the prom' in front of Martello Tower, West End. Over the years the site grew very fast and more friends were made."

"On spare ground behind the huts we would play games, rounders, football, "huck a buck". We cooked meals, ran backwards and forwards into the sea, loads of us in those days."

"Sundays seemed special for everyone, as in the afternoon you would hear a voice calling out: "shrimps, shrimps, fresh off the boat, 2d a pint."

"Almost everyone would run in and out of the huts to find the man with his cycle and large basket, with the colanders, buy and then run to the tap to wash them and enjoy them with bread and butter for tea. Some thought it was a messy teatime, but in those days it was fun abound."

"If anybody had a birthday, folks all around would join together and have a party, sitting around on rugs and all joined in."

"Then in 1939 war came, and I received a letter from the War Department to say if the hut was not removed it would be taken over by the forces and used as they wished. After that two and a half years of real pleasure, my

Butlin's Amusement Park (later Manning's) at Felixstowe as it was in the 1930s with a 'monkey island'

world broke around me."

" I spoke and asked advice form Mr. Bundall who I had bought the hut from and he, being a gentleman, came to my aid. He brought it back to Ipswich onto his land and said we could dig land around it and grow veggies, which the country was asking us to do "Grow For Victory" was the order of the day."

" When war was over I wrote to the council and asked if there was a chance of huts going back at any time and the answer came back: "Not along the Prom". Following that, Gerald Benjamin, an Ipswich House Agent in Elm Street, purchased land in front of Manor Terrace, on writing to him about a site, he answered he had several inquiries and I could have a site in the front row which was not quite close to the prom. He asked £1 holding

for one year and then I was allowed to have the hut taken back. So after a few years, older and happy again, we returned until we sold that when they started talking about a sea wall and my hubby and myself bought another. A bit more up-to-date, with a little cooker and lighting instead of the two oil-stores and candles we had used previously. This one was in the front row on Wireless Green, so we started all over again."

"They were wonderful times, no expense to pay out to have the fun and friends we had in all those years and only one break-in. It's a sore sight that end of the prom now, but the whole family have lovely memories, how times have changed."

School Days

Ink wells, a bottle of milk every day, receiving humiliating beatings in front of your friends, all memories of school in the past. Comforts were few and far between. Classes were often large with up to forty pupils to one teacher. Some were heated by open coal fires and lit by gas lamps. During the Second World War children had to try and concentrate on lessons often interrupted by air raids. Lessons sometimes continued in air raid shelters with staff and pupils clutching gas masks. Playgrounds were sometimes the sites of search lights and barrage balloons.

It was not until the 1980s that being punished with a cane was banned from school life for ever. Among the school featured in this section is Tower Ramparts Secondary Modern School in the town centre. It was where the Tower Ramparts Shopping Centre is now. There are colourful memories of life there and how the staff used the cane on a daily basis.

Tower Ramparts Cricket team in 1948. This images was supplied by Russell Berry.

Tower Ramparts School

Mike Sparks of King Edward Road, Barnet, saw a member of his family in the picture that we recently published. Mike said.

"I was at Tower Ramparts from 1953 until 1955 when my family moved to Barnet.

"it was certainly a violent place for newcomers – I was petrified when I moved there from Smart Street Primary, after failing my eleven plus. I was very quiet I can assure you, and miraculously avoided the dreaded stocks. They were a playground punishment in the school railing handed out by forth year boys. However, beatings up were commonplace and accepted, and you could get the stick from teachers for virtually anything, starting with just breathing! No one escaped the enthusiasm for corporal punishment displayed by some of the staff."

"In the winter the Headmaster Mr Heath would

have a roaring fire in his room and when you went there for punishment I seem to recall it was as hot as the pit of hell. This did not help. I well recall teacher Arthur Gillam and his famous cricket box worn over his trousers. He would wear this at break times when showing his batting skills in the playground nets. It is rumoured that he once put a ball through the fabric roof of his old Riley car."

"Harry Hacon was my last form master at Tower Ramparts. He carried a short cane up the sleeve of his jacket and would use it wherever and whenever he felt it appropriate. I recall

him caning the whole of our class once. Teacher 'Spud' Baker, I can still remember the wondrous phrases he would use at assembly to pick out some poor pupil, like, "Get out boy, you're a disease!" and how a chorus of voices would advise him to "Give him the stick, sir!"

"My form master for the first two years of my time at Tower Ramparts was a Mr Hipkin. He always seemed to have a problem with his eyes so his canings were sometimes inaccurately targeted."

"I was a member of the school choir which was run on a Friday afternoon by Mr H Bates Wilkinson who was

choirmaster at the Tower Church. I was in the choir for three years and we never performed anything for anyone as far as I can recall."

"Although it was, at times, a violent and troubled place, I found that when I moved to a Barnet School the quality of what I had learned at Tower Ramparts was actually streets ahead of what was then expected of me. I therefore coasted the final two terms of my education in a co-educational school which did not have corporal punishment."

School was a tough place for children in the 1930s and 40s, but you wouldn't be able to tell from these smiling faces.

Henry (left) and Frank Webb with their mother soon before she died, leaving them as orphans. Henry said, " I cannot remember when I first sensed that all was not well at home. I had a childish fear that something dreadful was about to happen. My mother's energy flagged, she quickly got tired, which was not like her. Her poor appetite failed altogether. She always insisted she would be all right, but she was not, her energy slowly sapped. Our mum was forty-six when she died. Her eyes were dark and never looked well She was tall and thin and tired looking. Through continuous hard work she was old before her time. In my early months and years at St John's I used to have dreams about her. Dreams where we were all together again as in the old days. I used to feel warm and very happy. We would all be together sitting in a garden".

To us there had always been a godlike quality about our mum. Lined and aged before her years perhaps but she always seemed indestructible.

St John's Orphanage

St John's Orphanage stood at the corner of Freehold Road and Bloomfield Street Ipswich. Henry Webb of Walsingham Court, Stoke Park, Ipswich was sent there with his twin brother Frank in 1932.

Henry and Frank Webb had a happy early childhood living with their widowed mother Jessie at 49 Ringham Road, Ipswich. Their mother managed to give the twins a normal upbringing for boys born in 1925. There were trips to the seaside with sandcastles and ice creams, birthday parties with children from neighbouring streets. At Christmas their mother managed to buy presents. Henry remembers starting school as his mother held the twin's hands on their first day. There were a few tears as they watched her vanish down the corridor. Little did the twins know what sadness was ahead. When they were seven their mother died.

Henry said "For most the halcyon carefree days of childhood come to an end by the gradual natural process of growing up. In our case instead of just petering out they went out with a suddeness that left such desolation and puzzling sadness behind as only those who have experienced it can understand."

"We were only one-year-old when our dad, Henry, Mum's second husband died of consumption (Tuberculosis) in the local sanatorium. Mum was left with Frank and I and two other children from her first marriage to bring up. For six years she struggled until the two eldest found work and were able to help with family finances. The years of struggle took their toll. By the time we were seven our mother who was the forty-six was dying of the disease herself. When she died we were committed to the care of the local council a the St John's home."

We soon found that we were to exchange the kindly and loving tolerance of home with it's tears of forgiveness for a life composed of strict discipline and harsh routine."

After mum's funeral we spent a sad few hours round the fire. All our thoughts were on tomorrow and our final bedtime was miserable for all. The memories of that last time we climbed those familiar old stairs come across the years sharp and bright with an old pain that has never been forgotten. After a while we blew out the candle but I could not sleep knowing that this time tomorrow we would be in a bed behind those strange walls of St John's. Brother Willie went to relations in Norfolk and sister Margery went to live with an aunt."

"Our pets, the wheelbarrow Granddad made, our home-made stilts, all looked neglected and forlorn in the corner of the washhouse yard on the grey wet November day in 1932 we went to St John's only a ten minute walk from our home."

"St John's home was the last of the many grim old barrack type orphanages which existed for decades before the Second World War. It was not a cosy foster home for children with all today's comforts. It was run like a remand home or prison. The homes were rough, hard and barbaric."

"The policy before the Second World War was for children to be placed in the care of council homes until they were fifteen. Then for them to have the choice of a working boys home in London or to join the armed services."

"There were thousands of children growing up in council care during the years between the two World Wars. Some were the result of family tragedy, or through poverty caused by unemployment or just neglect."

"When you were admitted to the home children from a family unit were split up and no direct daily contact was allowed between sexes, not even brother and sister. The only time you would see each other was in the dining hall, or at visiting times. Once a child became an inmate at a home he or she never saw much of the outside world other than school days or outings". Henry attended Clifford Road, California, and Whitton Open Air School."

"When you were taken into care you lost your identity and sense of belonging. You suffered great loneliness. I was never taken on anyone's knee or kissed and cuddled. We had to give up most of our treasured possessions."

"Discipline was harsh. If you fell out of line or misbehaved you were usually given a good hiding or some extra task like scrubbing, extra yard drill or heavy kitchen duties. The daily routine was of work and effort where each child had a number and followed a routine for that number."

"Saturday mornings were spent with two hours of army style drill, and marching in line and open ranks. There was also physical training. Every morning before school we had to make our beds, polish the floors, clear up the dining hall and wash up."

The daily sick parade at the home was mainly of boys who needed dressings changed for scraped knees etc. One of the masters would escort the "Sick Lame and Lazy" to the infirmary. I was quite often in the sick brigade because of a chronic bone complaint. This meant I would be admitted for a spell of complete rest which would mean a few weeks away from the scrubbing, bed

making, drilling or marching for a while. No more being bawled at by "Three Hairs" as we called Mr Roberts the boys senior officer. He was a strong, stocky, thick set, bow legged and practically bald with a few strands of hair which would fall over his eyes. For me those bouts of enforced rest could not come round quickly enough, or last long enough."

"Life at St John's did have some happy times squeezed between the routine and work. Hours spent in the yard on long summer days with our games and pastimes. Hours would be spent sorting through our collection of cigarette cards or reading comics. We would play leapfrog, touch, and have races, play rounders and football. Football with a real ball was not allowed (only on the playing field). We had a goal chalked on the wall and played with a rag ball held together with string or tape. In the autumn came conkers, and pop guns made from Elder wood."

Above all else reading was my favourite pastime and still is. Another treat was a weekly Tuesday evening film show, with films like, Tom Mix, and Buck Jones Westerns, and Will Hay, Robertson Hare, and Tom Walls comedies."

Christmas at St John's was much different from our family gathering. It was still the highlight of our year. It

was the most looked forward to of all our annual treats. The summer trip to the seaside was always enjoyable, also the yearly trip to the cinema or visit to the pantomime. To all of us in the orphanage the Christmas season was the peak of it all, compared to the rest of the year St John's became a fairyland. The officers relaxed the rigid discipline. For a time they became ordinary mortals."

"The institutional way of orphanage life I knew as a boy has gone forever. My generation was the last to experience it. It was harsh, drab with a stern code of discipline and routine. In our child minds we knew outside those high walls of St John's hundreds were on the dole, there was much poverty, children suffered malnutrition. At least we were sure of three meals a day, a good bed, and strong shoes on our feet".

"Strangely I now feel a great sense of nostalgia for that grim old place that is now mostly covered by houses and flats."

Life as a child in the 1930s

Pocket money was usually in short supply for children growing up before the more affluent days after the 1950s.

Swapping comics and cigarette cards, or gathering bottles to collect the deposit money from the shops, were all enterprising ways of saving and raising a little cash.

Bob Kessler of Needham Market lived in Alpe Street, Ipswich, from the age of six. He tells us in a wonderful, colourful way how life for

children in the 1940s. Bob was born in Woodbridge in 1936. Bob's father left the family at the start of World War Two.

Bob tells us of his life as a small boy living close to the Ipswich town centre. He said.

"My mother was a wonderful person and although having to bring us up on her own she managed superbly. Everyone had to do something to help. The shopping was my speciality from a very early age, my favourite being the butchers. Of course everything was on ration, with books of stamp coupons, which had to be presented for everything. Coupons were a carefully guarded commodity, being used for all manners of wheeling and dealing. Someone with a sweet tooth might trade his clothes coupons for your sweet coupons; all strictly illegal but a common practice."

"There was also the black-market which could supply almost anything at a price, and the people dealing in this way were treated as criminals if caught. Probably just as well we were poor or I might have been tempted into some illicit dealings!"

"It is my honest belief that one of the things, which helped the community to stay calm and collected in those times of great stress, was "queuing". The necessity of having to stand, sometimes for hours, in an orderly line in order to get things like bread and butter, was a real test for strength of character. Heaven help anyone who tried to "jump the queue" though."

"Bones were my speciality at that time and sounds strange I know, but to talk the butcher into parting with a marrow bone in those days was quite an achievement. Mother would boil these bones up for stock, soups, gravies and keep a stockpot

of stew, which would keep for many days having a thick layer of jelly-fat on the top. When reheated and a few extra vegetables added, the most marvellous meals could be made."

"Finances being the way they were, I had to make my own pocket-money, collecting newspapers to sell to butchers and fish-merchants for 3d (1.5p) a stone (14lbs or 6.5kg) or acorns and rosehips, in season, at 3d a bushel. The "bushel" was an old measure for dry weight by volume and quite a large basket!"

"Being able to distinguish edible fruits and plants in the countryside was a real bonus in those days. Blackberries and hazelnuts, mushrooms and chestnuts, sloes, bullace and crab apples and all manner of berries and herbs for cooking and wine making. I remember mother making great quantities of wine from just about everything you could think of: tea leaves, rose petals, elderberries, parsnips, beetroot, carrots, all the fruits of course, but best of all were dandelions. We used to have an annual pilgrimage to pick dandelion heads to make the wine and for weeks afterwards your fingers were stained bright yellow. The wines were excellent and a special treat for the children at Christmas or birthday celebrations ñ very potent, too!"

"A pocket-money maker in the season was spending all day picking blackberries or collecting chestnuts to sell round the doors at 3d for a 2lb jam jar full. The people were most particular too, and would not buy unless the goods were top quality. Another source of revenue and much pleasure and amusement, was the various games we played with marbles, coins, cigarette cards and conkers as well as the exchanging of comics."

"Marbles were played either in the gutter, having to strike the opponents marble to win it: or the usual way with a hole in the ground and after the first pitch having to flick the marble into the hole with your thumb. This could be played with several marbles or "alleys" as we used to call them."

"Various sizes and types had different values which had to be determined carefully before a game. Glass, porcelain, stoneware and even ball bearings were used. For example your opponent might say, "This is my lucky alley, large glass and nicely marked, you'll have to win it three times". Or, "If you win this one I want it back for two others." And so on, making up the rules as you went along. Cigarette cards were also very popular units of exchange and swapping, to make up those missing from sets was a serious business. Now, almost sixty years on, these sets are extremely valuable to collectors and hundreds of pounds are paid for rare sets."

"Games used to be played with "spares". Sitting at the kerbside near a wall and flicking the cards against the wall, trying to cover a pre-placed card or coin. The one to cover first takes all the cards used. During and after the Second World War (1939-45) the first American comics came on the scene via GI's stationed in England. Superman, Captain Marvel and Batman had never been heard of previously."

"Exchanging and selling comics was very big business. Beano, Dandy, Hotspur, Knockout and Film Fun especially were passed around, and the American ones had a value of two or three of the English comics at this time. Boys would save these for years and as they got older would pass them to younger brothers. Some quite large auctions took place in school break times. All these types of enterprise played a large part in shaping my knowledge of the world and have stood me in good stead in negotiations later in my life."

"Later on I used to go anywhere to find rubbish tips to collect old wine bottles which, when cleaned up fetched 1d each at Cowells wine store in

Pupils at the Wherstead Road School are pictured here in fancy dress. The image was kindly donated by Mrs Pearl Scott, who is second from right in the first row.

Ipswich. Another useful item was the humble treacle tin. There was a business in Handford Road run by a man named Oldring. He used to buy up all surplus paints from government sources in great drums and would pay 1d for a clean 1lb treacle tin and 2d for a 2lb one in order to re-pot and sell the paint. At this time you could not buy paint or wallpaper except from this type of business. With the basic Battleship Grey and Khaki type paints some weird colours were mixed."

"Shortly after the war when Martlesham Airfield was closed, all the cycles the airmen had used were smashed up and buried in a pit near Kesgrave. After letting the dust settle I took a spade and dug up enough parts to make several bikes which I sold for between £1-£3 each. What a fortune."

Priory Heath School

It was September 1938 when Priory Heath School opened its doors for the first time. The world was about to go to war and part of daily life at the school involved air raid training, how to use a gas mask and many other grim facts of preparing for the war, which was declared one year later.

Mrs. J Girling (nee Warren), recalls her time at the school during World War Two.

"The dreaded wail of the air-raid siren regularly interrupted the formative years of my schooling at Priory Heath Infants School. As five-year-olds starting school at the onset of war, we were surprisingly happy and adaptable to the upheavals of constant exits from the classroom to the shelter."

"Gas mask slung across our shoulder were the norm, as we made our way to school each day, although thankfully, the need to utilise those claustrophobic contraptions proved unnecessary."

"A special memory for me was a rather poignant one, as I had been chosen to play Red Riding Hood, primarily because I was the proud owner of a coat with a hood! Just as we were about to begin, the siren sounded, and we were promptly marched out to the shelters and I never did get to play that part, much to my dismay and that little scenario seems to have etched itself upon my memory!"

" My first classroom was painted bright yellow I recall. One of the highlights of the day would be story time when we would sit cross-legged on the floor around our teacher, eagerly listening to her reading us a story at the end of each day. She knew how to handle us, because prior to the story, she would pass a bag of boiled sweets around, which were eagerly accepted, and of course kept us quiet at the same time!"

"We regularly marched into the playground to proudly salute the Union Jack on special occasions, particularly Empire Day, instilling patriotic allegiance to young hearts and minds."

"I became Head Girl in my final year and one of my tasks was to deliver registers to each classroom and inform teachers if there was to be a school assembly that morning. If Miss Woods had forgotten to tell me, I would say whatever came into my head and was often standing in trepidation in the hall, waiting to see who had turned up! I'm sure I caused considerable confusion in the process! However, I remember being presented with a special prize at the end of my time at Priory Heath Infants School, so I couldn't have been too bad!"

"The past is important for all of us, shaping our futures in the process and hopefully helping us to learn from our mistakes and build on our successes."

"The school had an extremely good academic record in that era. I recall that about 60 per cent of the pupils in Class 4A passed the 11 plus in my year and the previous year, and it was the responsibility of Mrs. Perkins to get us through it. She was an excellent teacher with very strong disciplines and used the cane to good effect."

The football team at Priory Heath.

May Day has alway given children the opportunity to have some fun, here they dance around the May Pole and one lucky girl gets to be Queen for a day.

Northgate School

O.K Class, I want a short essay on "My Wartime Memories of Northgate School". I felt a bit like a schoolmaster reading through the responses to the look at life in the late 1930s and 1940s at this popular Ipswich school.

Ken Bean, of Dales Road, Ipswich wrote, " I was a pupil throughout the war from 1940 - 1945 in class (1A2). I should have gone to Northgate a year earlier, as I earned the equivalent of the 11 plus exam at St. Helen's school in 1939, but because I was too young, I was sent to Tower Ramparts for a year. We lived at 48 High Street then and although my younger brothers and sister were evacuated to Wolverhampton, my parents decided keep me here, to continue my Northgate School education. My best friends throughout the war were Bernie Eade, son of the hairdresser in High Street, we meet infrequently now and Ted Payne, then of Alderman Road, now unfortunately deceased."

"It amuses me now, although not at the time, I recall getting several painful lashes of the cane on my hands from headmaster Alfred Morris for supposedly covering the desk of teacher Mr. Tom Bishop with loads of soil.

"There was a barrage balloon in our playing field which was raised frequently during raids to avoid attacks by low flying planes, as we scampered to the air raid shelters. Between raids, I do admit now, those shelters, partly underground, were of use occasionally to foster friendships with the neighbouring girl's school!"

"The bomb that dropped alongside our form room was one of a string that dropped along the Sidegate Lane area, which I seem to recall, most did not explode. As a boy, I was most interested to run up High Street and Henley Road to view the result of the first bomb of the war, which dropped, in Dale Hall Lane, Ipswich, near to my present home."

"With the sound of the air raid siren, my brothers having returned from evacuation and I were running from Christchurch Park and down High Street when a bomb exploded on St. Margaret's Green. A piece of shrapnel took off my brother Ray's shoe heel as he ran. The shrapnel later on was recovered as a souvenir, and incidentally the heel too, to be nailed on again in those hard times."

"It was much later in the war that our talented school chum Gordon Hook was killed as a result of the first German jet-propelled aircraft raid on Britain, with most of the school attending the burial at the nearby cemetery. With the European War ending, several of us at Forestry Camp at East Harling beyond Thetford, cycled back to Ipswich to celebrate VE day on the area, now the bus terminus, between Tower Ramparts school and the Cricketers Public House." (See pic on p113)

Peter Goodman of Mayfield Road, Ipswich added, "I was at Northgate from 1937 to 1943 I can recall all members of staff and their idiosyncrasies. Like dear Mr. Litchfield who was renowned for drawing attention to an explanation of a mathematical problem with "watch the board fella - I'm going through it! His class gave this bald-headed gentleman a hair brush and comb for a retirement present!"

"Then there was Rev Yates, the French teacher, who always wore two overcoats and somehow mounted his bicycle via an extended spindle of the rear wheel. Tom Bishop, whose bark was far worse than his bite and who would let us have a sleep during his geography lesson after a night much disturbed by an air raid. Also the master, who shall remain nameless, with his widely known affinity with the Royal George!"

" Despite all the wartime problems we all considered (and still do) that the local education system was pretty good."

Dennis Green said, "I was a Northgate boy from 1935 to 1941, although the last six months were spent in the sixth form at Alderman Newton's School, Leicester. My wife Barbara (nee Eaton) was a Northgate girl from 1941 to 1946."

"Trenches were not the only things we dug. After taking our General Schools Exams we spent many hours throwing up earthworks around the searchlight battery along Humber Doucy Lane. As a reward the soldiers would let us look at some of their magazines. What would mum have said?"

"I think the examiners must have been generous in 1940, as we were the first wartime examinees. I managed to gain exemption from

Matriculation, but didn't really know what it meant."

"An air-raid two thirds of the way through the French exam meant that we headed for the shelters and were not allowed back into the exam. I got a pass. My prayers were not answered in the Physics exam. No raid – I failed."

Pearle Cook (nee Foster) added,

"I was a pupil there in 1932, previous to that I had been at school in Bolton Lane for four years – when Miss Marjorie Jarrett was headmistress. She was still there as Head when I went to Northgate where I only spent one year."

"I can recall Miss Debenham, who taught us Maths – an excellent teacher, but very strict, but who nevertheless had a wonderful sense of humour!"

I went to the Northgate from Rosehill School, Derby Road in 1941."

"I lived in Orwell Road then and used to cycle to school, and home to lunch – Cauldwell Hall Road and Sidegate Lane would be full of cyclists every morning and late afternoon."

"The boys' school was divided into houses also – Collingwood, Duncan, Grenville, Nelson, Rayleigh and Rodney – all the athletic types were in Grenville and non-athletic

type like me – 10 stone "Fatty" Bloomfield – went into Collingwood. Amazingly I loved sport, played First Division tennis and still play squash at 71!"

"There are so many memories – one of the oddest was we were running towards the shelter – this would be towards the end of the war and a doodle bug was flying above us – the engine stopped and it headed one way and we all ran back to the school."

"Amongst the best and most frightening teachers were Mr. Hotham (Mathematics) and Mr. Bishop who taught geography and handwriting."

"We had Mr. Hatham for three periods of mathematics on a Wednesday afternoon in my last year – he was a great teacher but strict – not the best of afternoons. Mr. Bishop taught geography and also handwriting, it was amazing that on our leaving day at school we queued up to say goodbye to Mr. Hatham and Mr. Bishop – whom we dreaded in our days there."

Ray Pilgrim said "Both my wife and I were pupils at Northgate. We left the Ipswich area in 1960 and have since lived in Yorkshire, Merseyside and Lancashire, where I have worked as a lecturer in marine radio and radar. It is interesting to note that in my last post at The Nautical College, Fleetwood where I was Head of

Pupils in a carpentry class at Northgate Boys School in around 1930. This was a particularly useful lesson for students and provided useful skills for the future.

Department, two of my lecturing staff of 23, were ex-Northgate boys."

"David Larter and Andrew Hodder, neither of whom I had met before, were at the school in the 50s and 60s. Also, the manager of the local Marconi depot, John Dallaston, had also been at Northgate, but in the 20s. We all agreed that we were grateful to Northgate for giving us an excellent education."

"I have lots of memories of those wartime days, both at Leicester and Sidegate Lane, and one in particular I must relate. A certain Dennis Collins, who I think started in 1937, was renowned for being an inventor of madcap pranks.

One morning a large load of mattresses were delivered and dumped on the concrete below the chemistry lab, which was on the second floor of the building. I think the purpose of the mattresses was for the use by staff on fire-watching duties, which they were obliged to carry out when the school was unoccupied. Towards the end of lunchtime, Dennis, having an eye for a bit of business, passed his cap round promising that when sufficient cash had been collected he would jump off the flat roof of the chemistry lab."

"This was successfully accomplished and much to the delight of the many onlookers he repeated this escapade, slipping in a

somersault or two for good measure. However, in the middle of his third jump, around the corner came dear old Mr. Cusworth, returning gracefully on his bicycle from what one must assume to have been a leisurely lunch. They appeared to have spotted each other simultaneously and the result was hilarious. Dennis tried to claw his way back up an imaginary ladder and Mr. Cusworth rode straight off the rather high concrete path onto the tennis courts."

"Fortunately neither were injured apart from Dennis when Aflie exercised his right arm a little later."

An aerial shot of Northgate School, Sidegate Lane West runs across the picture. The fields were marked out for rugby.

A group of female pupils at the Northgate Grammar school line up here.

Wakling's bakery shop at the corner of Albion Street and Fore Hamlet.

Shopping

Before the 1960s there were no supermarkets and housewives had to shop for fresh produce on a daily basis as few home had a refrigerator.

Small local businesses thrived with each housing estate having a full range of shops. A butcher, baker, grocer and greengrocer operated within walking distance of most homes selling mainly local produce. Many small shops also operated a delivery service by a lad with a bicycle.

Larger items were purchased in the town centre of Ipswich. Few people would travel to another town to buy anything. Trading at every level was much more localised than today. In the 1930s even the trolley bus fleet was produced locally by engineering company Ransomes Sims and Jefferies.

Shopping in the 1930s

As World War Two came to an end imported fruit like bananas and oranges returned to the shops and children were able to enjoy them for the first time. This great image shows the strange new fruit being sampled by a couple of youngsters.

Banana, this beautiful fruit is available every day in our shops and supermarkets. Its fresh sweet and unique flavour is largely taken for granted by us all. There is a generation who, when they were children during the Second World War, only heard stories of such exotic items from across the world. Importing fruit was a long way down the list of the country's needs during the war years of 1939 to 1945.

Mary Clay (nee Fletcher) wrote to me from Yuba City, California USA. "Reading about the first bananas in the shops after the war reminded me of the day I came home from school and saw my first one. I was eight years old and my mum was out. The beautiful surprise was lying in the middle of the kitchen table. I quickly peeled it and gobbled it up. When my mum came home a little while later she asked if I'd seen the banana and I said, "Yes, I ate it and it was delicious". She looked at me with a horrified expression and told me that was the only one she could find and we were all going to share it. I was terrified, as I knew I was in deep trouble. Then she started grinning and I knew she had more hidden away and was only teasing me. Whew! What a relief that was. It sure made my first taste of bananas memorable; I'll never forget it. I also remember when sweets finally went off the ration and the jars of sweets disappeared overnight off the shelves of the shop at the corner of Bramford Rd. and Chevalier Street near our home. I believe the Government had to put sugar back on ration for a while longer as there was

Staff in their smart uniforms outside the Vernon Street Co-op store in the 1930s The Co-op stores were incredibly important for both business people and the general populace of the town. They offered a huge range of products at reasonable prices.

none to be had because the public went mad buying all they could after going without for so long. It's all so hard to imagine nowadays."

Blue paper bags filled with sugar, being surprised to see bananas for sale in Ipswich, fish and chips with lashings of salt and vinegar. A great mix of memories all prompted by one photograph of a corner shop in Bramford Road, Ipswich, which belonged to Jessie Steel.

Rita Wheeler, (nee Thurlow) of Stratford Road, Ipswich, lived in Bramford Road with her family. Rita said "We lived at number 18 just across the road from Mr Steel's shop, mum, dad and five of us children. I remember in the 1940s being sent over to get odd groceries, especially sugar, which was kept in a big sack. It was weighed out with a big shiny scoop and put into blue bags, I used to love looking at the jars of

sweets. A few come to mind like aniseed balls, locust beans, liquorice roots, that you chewed like wood to get the juice out and lemonade crystals. We only had sweets once a week, when mum got the weekly groceries and they had to be shared between all of us."

"Mr Steel used to make up bags with a square piece of paper, fold it into a cone shape and twist the bottom so the contents wouldn't fall out. When I go past there

Shops on Bramford Road

now I look at the old street (which is now flats and houses) and think what happy days we had there".

"Next door to Mr Steel was Mr Pilley the barber. The next road down was Bulmer Road, on the corner was Mr Gedge the shoe repairers. You could smell the leather as soon as you walked in the door and watch while he soled and heeled the shoes and put "blakeys" (steel tips) on so they would last longer."

"Opposite was the Co-op, we would take the order book in to have the weekly groceries made up. The assistants would put the money in a tube, pull a handle and the tube would go across the ceiling to the office in the corner."

"On the corner of Rendlesham Road was Bickers shop, we took the accumulator for the radio to be charged up so we could listen to the serials like "Dick Barton, special agent".

Jenny Laughlin, of Fraser Road, Bramford., grew up in Prospect Road, Ipswich, and can recall many of the local businesses in Bramford Road. Jenny said. "For me as a child Bramford Road was the hub of the community of all the roads that went off it, from Wilberforce Street to Gatacre Road. I was brought up in Prospect Road and can remember many of the shops. All the shops you needed were there, Co-op, Bickers cycle shop, where you took the accumulator on a Saturday morning to be

charged up for the wireless. There was Harvey, greengrocer, J C. Ottley, butcher, Maureens Ladies' hairdressers, Colin Robinson's paper shop on corner of Victoria Street."

"On the other side of the road was Garner's fish and chip shop. When we were children there was a box kept in the corner to stand on, as we couldn't see over the counter. We asked for three penneth of chips with scraps, salt and vinegar – old Mr Gardiner used to say 'Don't want much for 3d do you? There was Miss Elliman's haberdashery shop, which sold everything you could think of. Next was Cranes selling bacon – cold meats and a bit of groceries – then the junk shop. There was Southgate's greengrocery, where we saw our first bananas, someone called out while we were playing in the street, "Southgate's have got bananas in the window". You have never seen children run so fast, all pushing each other to see them. Next door was Bilner's junk bookshop. On the corner of Prospect Road was the grocery store run by two nice sisters, Lily and Olive Roberts, with the sweets in little glass dishes in the window. Sugar was put in blue bags curled round their hands to make a cone shape, next to them was Burrow's pork butchers then French and Plowman, wet fish shop. Nearby was Clancie's paper shop and Newstead bakers, where if lucky, you could get a stale cream split for a penny on the way to school."

"Angels haberdashery, with big black blinds, was on the other corner, another haberdashery shop, then Fountains fish and chip shop, Hales chemists was all dark wood and big coloured bottles, then the Salvation Army hall (still there). Mrs Hampton's antique shop, you

could buy secondhand furniture there. There was the International Stores, then Bramford Road School, and the post office and Spurgeon's sweet shop. There was every shop you needed, so no need to go to town. Also everyone helped each other in those days."

"At the junction with Norwich Road was the Rose & Crown pub. Opposite Bickers shop was the Staff of Life, on the corner of Wellington Street was the Three Cups, then the Spotted Cow, looking down Prospect Road. So plenty of drinking holes, as the saying goes!"

"The single decker trams turned at Adair Road. When we went to Westbourne School we used to ride them for 1d, We only used the tram when it rained. Usually we had to walk to school, but we had happy days, no one had much money but we were all in the same boat in the years after the Second World War."

"Most of the little terraced houses and pubs and shops are gone but they are happy childhood memories. There are still shops on Bramford Road, but not as we knew them."

"Joan Reed of Allenby Road, Ipswich, has special memories of Jessie Steel's shop. Joan said. "How nice to see Jessie Steel's shop in the Evening Star, I was born there, my mum and dad rented rooms over the shops. I was born in 1925 and spent my childhood days there, just past Steel's was Wells Hairdressers, Potter's general store, who made delicious meat pies and ice cream, really yummy, then Shorts shoe shop."

"I used to walk to Bramford Road School in Gatacre Road. We used to have a penny to spend at Roberts's sweet shop further down Bramford Road. We would get a cone shape bag full of sweets for our penny. When I was older Mr Steel used to let me help in the shop, and Sunday night he gave us a little treat of sweets."

"I had to walk from Steel's to Westbourne School. No transport to and from in those days. Later I worked on the Ipswich buses as a "clippie". I later met my late husband Stanley who also worked on the buses. We married and started our married life above Steel's shop and also cared for my parents."

A 1930s Christmas

Chickens kept in the garden, reared from tiny chicks, were prepared for the Christmas Day feast in many homes until the 1960s, when there was a little more cash around to buy oven ready birds from a butcher.

Chicken was a special treat, only eaten on high days and on holidays. I was born in 1946 unaware in the 1950s just how tight the family budget was. Many small back gardens had chickens that provided eggs and a nice plump bird for Christmas Day.

They were reared on a diet of kitchen scraps mixed with chicken meal. My father had the awful job of killing the bird (out of sight of the family) and preparing it for cooking. Mum took over in the kitchen and our family of four enjoyed a great roast with all the traditional vegetables.

Buying an oven ready bird was, I suppose, beyond the budget in the difficult economic times after the Second World War. Other winter memories of tasty home food include making

toast on an open coal fire with a special fork kept by the fireplace. There was nothing quite like the smoky toast with a layer of beef dripping! My family laugh at me now, they think I am making it all up!

For those who are not familiar with the delights of dripping it was the fat from roast meat kept cold in a bowl for use later. It was very nice, honest!

Joyce Garnham of Warren Heath, Ipswich, was born in Gipping Street, Ipswich and was also a fan of "dripping". Joyce explains.

"We had the biggest family in the area, but we were the best dressed and fed. I well remember our Christmas times, we always had a present each and a stocking, one of mother's old ones. We used to hang them around the fireplace before going to bed and mother used to fill them up with a few sweets, nuts, apples, oranges also a cracker and a new penny. We really thought we were rich. We also had a Christmas tree with sugar fancies and sugar mice, and our tummies were

really full with so much food. When we think about what we used to eat in those days, plum pudding, steak and kidney pudding and dripping on toast (lovely). Not one of us was fat in those days."

"I was born in Gipping Street, number seven of the Studd family. My earliest memories are of starting school at the age of four years at London Road school. We had a really small house in Gipping Street and soon after I started school my mother was allocated a council house in Landseer Road. My mother hated it. She didn't want to live on a council estate. We only stayed in Landseer Road a short time, and then we got a house in Curriers Lane, where we stayed for several years."

"Then the council built three large houses in Tanners Lane and we were given the largest one as our family had grown quite a lot by then. Some of the neighbours were really jealous."

"During the Second-World-War there had been an air raid on all day but it was very quiet, so mum sent me to

Marks and Spencer to get a Swiss roll for tea (such luxury). I went to Marks via the Mount and Blackhorse Lane, and decided to come back down Princes Street and when I was halfway down a German plane came over and I saw the bombs come out of the plane. That was when Paul's at the docks got a direct hit and one of my friends' little brothers was killed under all the grain. I ran as fast as I could home, although people kept shouting for me to lie down."

"I also remember there being a poor children's outing when business people and taxi drivers used to decorate their cars and lorries and take the children to a field at Wherstead for fun and games. Of course mother would never let me go, but my brothers did. Also there used to be a poor children's Christmas dinner at the Corn Exchange.

The only trip I went on was to a place called Maryland in Sproughton. We went on a bus and thought we went miles away."

"I was picked for this trip because I was in hospital for a spell after being scalded badly. I thought it was lovely, especially having a bed to myself. I think it was sort of convalescence and I remember having my birthday there so it must have been in June."

"When I was about twelve-

years-old, I used to do a paper round and one quiet Sunday morning I was cycling up Princes Street when suddenly a mass of soldiers came out of the train station, like nothing I had seen before. I rushed home to call my dad and said, "Come quick Dad, we are being invaded." But of course they turned out to be Americans."

"Later on when I was older and working at Smiths Suitalls (a high-class stationer) in the Buttermarket, the Americans used to come in for printed stationery. They were always teasing me and saying "Hi, Red" because of my hair and they used to ask me to go on a date but I never did."

"Two shops I remember from The Mount area of Ipswich were Miss Steven's where mother used to get her groceries. We used to collect it in an old pram; there was so much of it. The other shop was Mr Bumstead's, where mother saved a few coppers each week so we could have a nice Christmas. Also I think there used to be two other shops over the other side of the road and behind them was the mortuary (really creepy)."

"When my friends and I were about sixteen- years-old, the highlight of the week was when bus loads of Dutch sailors used to come

to Ipswich from Shotley. We all made friends with them."

"My friends were Maureen Dunnett, Joan Mills, Barbara Smith and Kathy Everett.

When we all went to the pictures with the sailors at the Regent we used to take up a whole row of seats. We used to have a laugh, as the Dutch boys spoke very little English they didn't understand much and with our Suffolk accent we were no help."

"In 1939 when Princes Street was flooded and men carried girls from Churchman's factory through the floods. The water came up Tanners Lane but not as far as our house. I was about eight years old at the time, and some horses got loose from somewhere and were very frightened and they came up our road and I screamed, which made the horses more frightened. The men trying to catch the horses called me some colourful names!"

"There was a cattle market on Tuesdays in the Princes Street area of Ipswich. I used to get scared when I came home from work at dinnertime in case there was a cow on the loose!"

Ronald Garnham was born at Stirling Street where he grew up with his parents in a family of nine. "Christmas time would bring a few presents, a new penny, an apple and orange, a few

Fun for all the family at Christmas time in Ipswich!

sweets and maybe one toy."

"My father, Walter worked in the demolition business. On Sundays he collected the newspapers from Ipswich Station and delivered them by Model T Ford to earn a little extra to help pay for things like a Christmas treat for his children. Christmas dinner was usually chicken, or sometimes rabbit pie."

"Like most homes the front room was kept for high days and holidays. We had a piano there where we would all gather round to sing carols and other popular songs."

They Don't Build Them Like That Anymore

Model steam trains in a shop window attract boys of all ages. There was a tiny shop in Friars Street; Ipswich where I would go to look in the window at beautifully made model trains. This shop was straight from a Charles Dickens story. I recall the shop from the mid 1950s when I was around eight or nine years old. In those days it was not unusual for boys to be in town with a friend. I would try to pluck up courage to go inside but there was something about the shop, which I can recall, being a bit spooky.

Memories from Geoff Tuffs of Willoughby House, Barbican London promoted this childhood memory for me.

Geoff visited the shop in the late 1940s when he too was around eight-years-old. He then lived in Heath Road, Ipswich and was a pupil at St John's Primary School. Geoff said. "When I was a boy in the 1940s I used to visit a shop called Louis George in Friars Street Ipswich, close to the town centre. I never established who Louis

George was, but I believe I was served by him. An enormous cap distinguished him, with the peak pulled well down, which he habitually wore. This character, at the time a relatively young man I would say, appeared to run the shop and he always served me."

"I recall he was of slight build, a nervous, unsmiling manner accompanied by a slightly high-pitched voice. His clothes, old and well worn, gave him the sort of shabby genteel appearance. He was pure Dickensian."

"What sort of shop was Louis George? I find it difficult to say exactly. It catered mainly, I think, for schoolboys with hobbies, so at least part of its stock consisted of things of a boyish mechanical nature: model steam engines, electrical circuits, small gauge train wheels, even the locomotive itself. What I do remember is the touching individuality of the shop. The layout of stock in the window was painstaking but amateurish, each item neatly

captioned, and on the door was a large card illustrating a selection of the merchandise contained within."

"I am unable to recall individual items, but I clearly remember that each one was drawn in pencil or ink with the same painstaking care as those objects displayed in the window. This card, in all the time I knew the shop, was always attached to the inside of the door."

"At that time, I collected cigarette cards. Although their issue had ceased at the beginning of the war, there were still plenty available in the years following 1945. I used to go to the shop to buy whole sets of cards. I only possessed a small number. The fact that I was able to obtain a pristine set of Churchman's 'Story of Navigation' for two-shillings and six-pence when before I had laboriously acquired only fourteen cards in various sorts of condition out of a series of fifty, was for me simply amazing."

"You entered the shop to a small area before a high

Albert List's cycle shop in Carr Street, Ipswich with manager Stanley Girling at the door. Cycling was hugely important to Ipswich at that time. It was normal to see thousands of bicycles flooding the streets as men and women made their way to work.

counter; there was so little stock there was nothing on which to browse! This thoroughly unremarkable interior has for me two abiding memories. It had a musty smell I can remember to this day. "

"While being served by whom I must call Louis – I could see into a small back room or parlour. There, with his white head bowed, was an old man intently working on something that was always out of my vision. Possibly, he was carefully preparing the next illustrated card to go on the shop door. I always assumed he was the father and his son served me."

What stays with me is the pathos of that little interior scene. The small shop and its two occupants were an intrinsic part of my childhood and an abiding curiosity remains with me."

Ipswich Shopping

There was a time, in quite recent memory, when almost every shop was shut on a Sunday. I can recall the frustration of being half way through a DIY job and running out of something simple like filler or one brass screw. Driving round town hoping to find somewhere that might have the items in stock so the job could be finished.

The other odd thing was to be able to see the item you needed in a corner shop, which had opened on a Sunday, but not being allowed to make the purchase. Now we can buy anything we want on a Sunday.

David Huxley of Piccadilly Close, Birmingham, remembers a great little shop, which was close to Stoke Bridge.

David said, " I was an Ipswich resident between 1964 and 1976. I grew to love the town and Suffolk as well. There was an ancient hardware shop that stood on the corner of Dock Street and Vernon Street until the area was redeveloped in the late 70s or early 80s.

"It was owned by a rather grumpy gentleman who knew where any item he had in stock was located in what was a very crowded and chaotic shop. He always seemed to be open on Sundays and to have what I wanted. The only trouble was he was slow finding it and very inclined to lecture his customers on their wicked ways. Many of the items in stock were rusty and he would always say, "They would clean up well".

"When the shop was demolished the stock must have been scrapped or sold off to a dealer. There were so few customers there that it could never have been sold over the counter. Another godsend shop in those days was Double's at Bourne Bridge - it never seemed to close".

Sally Newman wrote from her home in America. Sally has memories from the 1950s of a shop, which was near St Mary's Church in Elm Street.

Sally said. The stories of Louis George's shop in Friars Street reminds me of another curiosity shop of

sorts, on the Mount area, just along from St. Mary at Elms Church. Mr. Eastman's I think it was called. His shop was like nothing I had ever experienced before or since. Initially, to this child's eye, the shop interior appeared square. The large beamed ceiling was very low. The walls were made of some kind of large rock or bricks. The floor was cobbled or brick, it was noticeably uneven. There were large wooden tables facing you, neatly piled with all sorts of clothing. Everywhere you looked, above, below beside, hung, stacked and stored, there were merchandise.

There was a curious mix of smells, besides fusty and damp there was the smell of new clothing, leather and old tobacco."

"My memories of Mr Eastman are from the 1950s when I was about six or seven years old. He himself was an elderly, stooped, short, knarled sort of man. He used to write notes and numbers on cigarette papers."

"This is where I, as a young child growing up in Quadling Street, would on occasion be taken begrudgingly (money was hard to come by at times) by a relative, usually an aunt, for some basic school wear such as plimsolls, slipper bag. Maybe the odd pair of navy gym bloomers. All of which had to be larger sized than you needed for future growth. You had to smile... .thank goodness I still do."

TOP The Lloyds Avenue entrance to the popular town centre store of Footman Pretty and Company as it was in the 1930s. The site is now occupied by Debenhams store.

ABOVE The Buttermarket, Ipswich from Princes Street in January 1949. The street, now pedestrianised, was then open to two way traffic and parking.

Action from Ipswich Town Football Club around 1932. Ipswich then played in blue and white striped shirts. The wooden "chicken run" stand in the background remained at the ground until the 1970s.

Sport

The days of heavy leather boots and ball used in armature football are recalled in the team groups featured in this section. Ipswich Town Football Club was an armature club until 1936 and their ground was also home to many other sports including cricket, athletics to tug-o-war.

There are also memories of the Ipswich Lads Club who played many sports under the encouraging eye of the Ipswich Borough Police Force who organised teams as part of their involvement in the community

There are memories too of greyhound racing held off Bramford Road. These events made enterprising use of an old car engine to pull the "hare" round the track.

Lad's Club

A photograph of a young boxer brought memories of the days when clubs met at local pubs and the town's police force were active in training young fighters.

Maureen Betts of Bixley Road, Ipswich said "I recognise my Father Sid and grandfather Tom Southgate. They lived in Bond Street, Ipswich, and my father fought in the period around 1930."

Bill Southgate was in the Army during World War Two and became a prisoner of war in Burma.

David Ashford of Belstead Road, Ipswich, has sent me some information about Doug "Smiler" Perkins. He tells me Smiler, a former professional, was still teaching boxing in Ipswich in his seventies, apparently still doing a great performance with a skipping rope! He used to help Frannie Peak organise the Ipswich Amateur Boxing Club events.

Another well known locally based fighter was George "Squibs" Whitfield of Frampton Lane, Ipswich. George was born in Ferry Hill, County Durham in March 1920. In 1936, at the age of sixteen, he came to Ipswich to seek work with his brothers-in-law, Jack and Ruben Friese. All three Jordies started work at Cranes Engineering in Nacton Road, Ipswich. After serving in the Royal Navy during World War Two, George returned to South Shields to seek work, but soon to returned to Ipswich and Cranes where he trained the football team and boxed for the company. He also fought at the Public Hall in Westgate Street and St Matthews Baths Hall.

George tells me "In 1946 I turned professional, with fights all over East Anglia, the Midlands, London and the Home Counties. In 1948 I stopped fighting professionally. I was keen to remain active in the sport so joined the Ipswich Lads Club as a trainer, with two other ex-professional boxers, Vic Brooks and Vic Price."

"The early days at the club were above the Feathers Public House in Westgate Street, Ipswich, eventually with the support of the Ipswich police we got a purpose built gym in Arcade Street."

"Here with the well respected and remembered Sergeant Sutcliffe, many young boys were to have a memorable youth with the Ipswich Lads Club."

"There was a chance for

Ipswich boxer Doug "Smiler" Perkins was one of the finest amateurs in the area. He built a reputation as a tough fighter amongst a large group of promising boxers that came from the Ipswich area. "Smiler" retained a love of the sport, and was still coaching into his 70s.

thousands to watch boxing at the Co-op Fete on Christchurch Park. The ring and changing marquee was sited close to the Round Pond. With my fellow trainers I would be second to local boxers proudly fighting for their club. Some of the fighters locally I recall are, Mike Olden, Geoff Sparrow, Percy Lloyd, Mervin Dwyer, and Noel Kearney". From 1970 George, with boxing in his blood, helped to establish and run the Ipswich Ex-Boxers Association, where he was chairman when he retired in 1997."

Mrs. E Osborne, recounted her husband's boxing days."

"Robert James Osborne was a member of the Ipswich Lads Club and a very good young boxer in his time. Bob, as he was known, joined the club with George Gibbs and Sid Sutcliff who became Sgt. Sutcliff in the Ipswich Police. Nat Shaw was involved in the promotion side of boxing and used to take the boys to the various venues."

"Bob was a plumber and heating engineer by trade. He enlisted in the Royal Navy during the war and was working in the engine room of a ship that repaired other ships at sea."

TOP Ipswich boxer Sid Southgate with his father and trainer Tom around 1930. After a long period working at the docks, Sid Southgate enjoyed success as a professional boxer, fighting all over the country.

The Feathers Hotel, now demolished, at the corner of Lady Lane and Westgate Street, Ipswich in 1949. In its early years the Ipswich Lads Club used to meet there.

Ipswich Town FC were obviously the most popular club in the town, but there were also a number of good amateur teams at the grassroots level. The Ipswich Lads Club football team for 1948 is show here. They are, from the left back row, PC Rocket who managed the team, B Smith, F Tibbenham, B Sharman, D Keeble, and R Southgate. Front row; W Lilley, R Trenter, D Knights, L Baker, R Marsh and C Bullard.

Football in the 1930s

Today football is live on television. Football fans could only dream of such coverage in the 1950s. Few had a television and outside broadcasts were in their infancy at the BBC, the only channel broadcasting to our area. Certainly if you wanted to see Ipswich's matches home or away you had to be there.

Local derby matches between Ipswich Town and Norwich City are always passionate affairs.

Swede (right), a popular character at the club, gets the crowd going an Ipswich Town home match at Portman Road

The Whitton football team for the 1938-39 season. The differences in the sport between then and now are significant and some of these differences can be seen in this image. A heavy ball, sturdy boots and thick clothing all made the game tougher and slower than it is today.

It is interesting to note that Ipswich played in vertical blue and white stripes, when they were an amateur club.

"ST MARY ELMS" JUNIORS, FC, WINNERS IPSWICH JUNIOR LEAGUE, 1932-33.

The St Mary Elms Juniors Football Club, Ipswich who won the junior league for the 1932-33 season. St Mary Elms were a successful local team for many years.

Jimmy McLuckie, the Scottish international and leads his team out from the changing rooms. He joined the club in July 1936, made 57 appearances before leaving the club in July 1947.

Greyhound Racing

Tales of shady happening's at the Greyhound track in Ipswich come from Harold Cutter of Stratford Court, Ipswich. Peter Rogers had recalled earning his pocket money walking the dogs' back in the 1930s.

Harold told me a little more of the Greyhound racing in the Bramford Road area. With some "tricks of the trade" and interesting devices to propel the "hare" for the dogs to chase.

"I was born in Waveney Road in 1916 and can remember the Greyhound racing track that was where Eustace Road and Broadmere Road are now."

"In the early 30s round about 1934 to 1936 I owned a greyhound which I used to enter at this track. The hare was "propelled" around the track by means of a rope that was attached to a rear wheel of a jacked up car, the tyre had been removed and this formed the winding mechanism!"

"The "hare" was actually a bundle of rags and it's speed around the track was dependent on the man whose foot was on the accelerator. It wasn't unknown for the car to break down, the dogs catching up with the hare and total pandemonium ensuing."

"I can remember that my dog always got excited at the sound of the bell to start the race. This was a very good thing to be if the dog was already in the trap waiting the off. On one occasion we were outside the race area when my dog heard the bell, slipped his lead, jumped the fence and joined the race, which by this time was well underway! The best thing was that he caught all the dogs up and came in first."

"I can remember a slightly dodgy episode when I was asked, by another owner who I shan't name even after 70 years, to feed my dog up very well before the next race meeting. In effect "nobbling" him for that session. The reason was that the following week I could get better odds from the bookies since they would think my dog was on poor form."

"I wasn't happy about doing this knowing that if my father found out that even at eighteen I would still get the wrong side of his hand! Still boys will be boys so I asked my mother to make a large rice pudding for the dog under the pretext that I had been told that it was good for the dog and fed him the whole lot at the appropriate time."

"Needless to say I didn't back my dog. My father however, was loyal to the family and did so. I couldn't tell him not to for obvious reasons and to my utter amazement my dog came in first."

"The other owner accused me of not stuffing my dog as per the arrangement and his comments on hearing that I had fed it rice pudding were unprintable. Eventually the track closed down after the modern stadium was built in London Road which had all the amenities but not the atmosphere of the Bramford Lane track."

Bob Osborn of Felixstowe Road, Ipswich, also recalled the old car used to pull the "hare" round the greyhound track."

"In the 1930s I lived on Bramford Lane and remember the dog track. A motor car with a plinth about thee feet of the ground with the off side rear wheel removed and a big reel fitted in it's place pulled the "hare" round." is today.

May 1945. A VE Day Part at St Thomas's Church Hall on Bramford Road.

Post War

When the Second World War came to an end there was much celebration as life seemed about to improve. There were street parties for Victory in Europe Day in May 1945 and again in the August when Japan surrendered.

Men started to return from fighting the war and return to their jobs and women went back to their then more traditional place in society.

There were many years of struggle ahead as families were reunited. Household budgets were tight and most had to "make do and mend". Children wore handed down clothes and woollen items were unwound and remade into something else. It was not until 1953 that rationing finally came to an end. It was at least another ten years before families could afford thing we all now take for granted like television, refrigerators, cars, telephones, central heating and holidays abroad.

Let's Party

Tucked away in cupboards all over the world are photographs of celebrations in and around Ipswich. The pictures are of the days everybody had waited almost six years for. Victory in Europe celebrations at the end of World War Two in 1945 saw the end of threats of bombing and destruction to homes in England. In August there was more jubilation as the war in the Far East came to an end. There was delight as family members were due home from war service.

Pat and Ken Butcher of Queensland, Australia, sent in a wonderful images as residents in Gorse Road gathered to celebrate.

Pat said, "Ken then lived in Rands Way. At the time he

Celebration Time in Austin Street where residents marked the end of the war.

was in hospital, but was allowed out to attend the party with his friend."

"At that time the roads were still busy with tanks and army vehicles constantly on the move. We had an air raid shelter in the garden near greengage trees. I often wonder if they are still there? It was damp and had lots of spiders, so was never used. My father was away in the navy so was rarely at home and my mother was of the opinion that if our number was up there was nothing

you could do so we mainly stayed in bed during the air raids."

"If things got really bad we all crowded into the cupboard under the stairs. The fact the gas meter was there did not seem to worry her! On the really bad nights we would go over the road to a big concrete shelter at the end of Glenavon Road. It was good fun as there were usually people there who either did not have their own shelter or were on their way somewhere and

needed shelter. My friend Drew lived nearby at number 97. I was impressed with the Morrison air raid shelter they had in their front room. On top of the shelter was his pride and joy, a model train layout."

"The shelters at school were always a good escape from lessons. Looking back it must have been a dreadful time for the poor teachers. I have never seen any mention of the Doodle Bug (V1 flying bomb) which fell in the fields close to Humberdoucy

Thousands attended this Victory in Europe party in the town centre. This area is now the town's bus station. In the background is Tower Ramparts School (formerly the Municipal Secondary School for Boys).

Lane. It cracked all our ceilings. We all went along the following morning to look and I clearly remember a policeman standing guard and stopping us picking up the pieces."

Pat and Ken moved to Australia with their two daughters in 1965 and on their last visit to Suffolk they were sad to see some of the changes. Pat said "When we were last in Suffolk we went to renew old memories, but what a lot of changes we found. The site of our old beach hut and the putting green at Felixstowe had gone. As children we spent our holidays at a caravan park near Beach Station, and used to walk along a beautiful leafy lane to the Dooley Pub, close to the old fort. There would be a beer for the adults and lemonade and a packet of crisps for the children."

A VE Day party in Coronation Road.

VE & VJ Celebrations

Marie Freeman (nee Croxon) of Bath sent me a picture from the Victory in Japan party in Coronation Road, Ipswich. It is packed with smiling faces of several generations.

Marie said "I was staying with my grandparents at the time as my home in South London had been damaged by a V2 rocket. My grandparents were Flora and Will Croxon of 6 Coronation Road, where they lived all their married lives. I had passed my scholarship exam for entry to the grammar school at Mitcham, but had to transfer to Northgate School for Girls, Ipswich for a few months. Apart from the food, the thing I remember most about the party was the fancy dress parade and the costume my grandmother obtained for me to wear."

Post-War Memories

Parts of Ipswich, which once were home to thousands of families, were cleared in the years after the Second World War.

Brian Dean, of Lower Faircox, Henfield, West Sussex, wrote to me with memories of a tragic event from his childhood in this part of town.

"In the summer of 1944, an army lorry full of troops ran out of control down Bishops Hill. It failed to negotiate the very narrow roadway in Fore Hamlet and overturned onto a group of schoolgirls making their way to Sunday School, causing fatal injuries to at least one of them as well as serious injury to both the others and the troops being carried on the lorry."

"I had left my home to visit my grandmother in Long Street a few minutes behind the girls, who had also set out from White Elm Street, and with whom I would otherwise have been walking and arrived on the scene just after the accident had occurred. A large crowd had already gathered to give help, including the crews and passengers of halted trolley buses."

Mrs. Wyatt had memories of her life in Romney Road, Ipswich.

"In the photo of Romney Road, VE Day party, I am the only adult in the front row. I will never forget the work which went into making it a day to remember when the whole street took part. The fun we had collecting spoonfuls of sugar, flour, jam and a few pennies, I supplied the eggs. My neighbour and I made 400 fancy cakes. We felt honoured when the mayor stayed to have a cup of tea and a cake."

"The Lairs, what memories my family have of the Lairs. Camping picnics, Pond Hall Farm, getting the water from the stream to make a cup of tea, the woods. Walking in the leaves, chestnuts, getting stuck in a tree. In winter when it snowed, happy days."

"I lived at 90 Romney Road; my garden was always full of my children's friends and their mums. I dug for victory, kept chickens, rabbits and turkeys. After the war my husband, who served in the RAF, worked for Cranes."

"My eldest son was born in Wingfield Nursing Home. The docks were bombed that day. I was asked, did I want to go to the shelter? I said not on your Nelly, I want to get rid of this lump on my belly!"

" My other children were born at 90 Romney Road. Nurse Frost was the midwife. My children went to Morland Road School, Landseer and Nacton. They attended Sunday School at All Hallows Church. We didn't think so at the time, but we lived a full, happy, friendly and helpful life. It was one for all, all for one. We exchanged vegetables and helped if anyone was sick; we looked after neighbour's children."

A VE Day party at Romney Road.

Hardships of Post-War England

If sometimes you think you are hard done by and wonder how you will pay for your holiday abroad or your car and all the luxury gadgets in your centrally heated home, just spare a thought for those who had to care for their family a couple of generations ago.

Work was hard to find in the 1930s. The world was suffering from economic depression and brave men who fought through the horrors of the First World War had to make ends meet for their families the best they could.

Bill Vince of Kensley Road, Felixstowe, told me how his father John returned to Ipswich, crippled in one leg from fighting for his country in France. With his wife and children to support John was allocated one of sixteen wooden former barrack buildings known as "The Hutments" built by the army on the edge of Ipswich close to where the Haven Hotel is on Felixstowe Road. They stood on an orchard which belonged to William Mayes, a market gardener, who was based at 479 Felixstowe Road.

Bill said, "I was born there in 1927. The huts each had four bedrooms and were built to accommodate around thirty men. There was a kitchen with a range where my mother worked hard to feed a large family. When we lived there my parents had five children. The huts were built in a semi circle with one outside gas lamp serving them all. They were also lit inside by gas lamps. We had great times as children making our own fun with a piece of rope and an old tyre hanging from the lamp post as a swing."

"My father's injury made it difficult for him to find work. He used to join crowds of men outside Crane's engineering works on Nacton Road hoping to get chosen for part time work. His main income was from emptying the outside toilets of the sixteen huts. Every day he would dig a trench and then collect the buckets from the "Bumbies" as the toilets were called."

There was one great plus to his work, his vegetable garden was wonderful! He produced prize winning crops which helped with the very tight family budget. Sometimes we children would take a trolley bus to town and visit Juby's butchers shop at the corner of Tacket Street and Foundation Street and exchange his home grown parsley for a few sausages or a piece of meat for the family dinner. We would often walk to the Salvation Army Citadel in Queens Way where we could buy a saucepan full of hot peas for one farthing. They were delicious."

"When the Gainsborough estate was built we were moved to a new house in Landseer Road, which was then unmade. I was then ten-years old. The huts were then demolished."

"At Landseer Road the family grew to eleven, including my parents. My brothers and sisters were, George, Joyce, Betty, Valerie, John, Keith, Michael and Rosie. There was no spare cash and Christmas presents were an orange, apple and a few nuts for each of the children. At birthday time I just received a card."

"I was a pupil at Priory

Heath and Landseer Secondary Modern Schools. My teachers at Landseer included headmaster "Polly" Perkins, Mr Broom, Mr English, Mr Norfolk, "Daddy" Collins, Mr Scott and Mr Davey. I have fond memories of my childhood. They were happy times; we made our own fun and did not feel we were missing out. It was just the way life was."

Ipswich was a barrack town until the 1930s when the main army base between Norwich Road and Anglsea Road closed. Permanent barracks for cavalry was built on that site in 1795. There were various sites built around town to accommodate men during times of conflict. The maltings close to Stoke Bridge were barracks during the Napoleonic wars. They are now converted to flats. At the same time there was a hutted camp built on Woodbridge Road just outside town for 8,000 men, this was called St Helens Barracks. The huts which Bill Vince lived in as a child were most likely built for First World War troops.

'The Hutments' in which Bill Vince and his family used to live are seen here in the background.

Victory Celebrations in the Town Centre

A group of mainly mothers and children throw their own VE Day Party, held in Harvey Street, Ipswich.

Sixty years ago celebrations of the end of the Second World War were in full swing in Europe as German forces surrendered and Victory in Europe was declared. Houses and lampposts were strung with bunting, and tables set up for one huge celebration. Pictures of that great day, when the dreadful conflict in Europe came to an end, are still coming to light.

The war in the Far East lasted until August when Japan surrendered, but at home thousands could celebrate that bombing raids were at last over and many servicemen could return to civilian life.

Rita Carro (nee Walton) sent a photograph from her home in Wanneroo, Australia of the VE party in Hervey Street, Ipswich May 5, 1945. Rita said "I was nine years old; it's me on the right standing up leaning on the table. My brother is second on the right sitting on the ground and my mother is standing at the back, on the right. I remember the VE Day party well, we all had a good time and we were very happy."

"In 1949, all my family came to Western Australia. We sailed on the "Dorsetshire". We left at 6.30pm from Liverpool; everyone was singing and dancing on the deck. We arrived in Fremantle on September 5. We had five weeks at sea, my father Leslie Walton was a good carpenter, and he had a good job to go to in Perth.

My father had worked in Ipswich at F Tibbenham's for 18 years, and then at Transport Motor Engineers Ltd, London Road, Ipswich as a coach builder. My mother, father and brother have all since passed away."

Brian Curtis, Australia, sent in a picture of a VE Day party in Bath Street, with residents pictured at the corner of Hawes Street. Reader's letters have helped to identify the scene.

Rosemary Mower (nee Ellinor) is at the front of the group, at the time she was staying with her aunt May Ellinor at 62 Bath Street, which is second house on the left. Her mother was in hospital and she lived with her aunt from the age of three until she was eight. She recollects there was a passage near that house leading to Harland Street where men would hurry through to the engineering works at Ransome's and Rapier when the "bull" hooter sounded for them to start their shift.

The celebration events at the ends of the Second World War proved so popular with residents of the Gainsborough estate they became an annual event for several years. This party group was at the Landseer Road, Labour Club in 1947.

Family Parties

A Victory in Europe party is in full swing here in Castle Road.

Party Time

Terry Blake of Evabrook Close, Ipswich was eleven when the war started and living in Dickens Road, Ipswich. By the time it ended he was in his early teens and in demand to play the piano at his local pub.

Terry said "I was just eleven-years-old when war was declared and about the only affect it had on me was to interrupt my piano lessons! I was one of those young people that liked the piano and was very disappointed that I was not allowed to continue my lessons.

I left school in 1942 when I was 14 to start work and still kept up my practice at the piano learning, as best as I could, to play the tunes of the day. The war produced so many lovely songs – many of which are still popular today."

"It wasn't long before I was asked to play the piano on a Saturday night at the local pub, The Handford Cottage, Handford Road, where I got a payment of a couple of shillings from the landlord plus the proceeds of a collection from the assembled company at the end of the evening. From time to time someone would come up to me and ask me to play a song so they could sing – most times they had no idea of the key they wanted me to play the song in – so I would say "you start - I'll follow..!"

"That proved to be a

VE Day parties took place all over the country in 1945. This one, from York Road, was obviously attended by a good number of people

wonderful "training ground" and I soon found that I could play anything that was required – provided someone could hum or sing it."

"Later on in the war years I played in various bands and then obtained a job as resident pianist at the Labour Club in Silent Street where each Saturday evening a concert was held and local artistes performed. Again this provided me with experience of playing the well-known songs and ballads of the day – very often from music I had never seen before. I was in

my mid teens at this time and one of the younger performers to play in those dark days of the war – I often wonder if any other of those who performed then are still alive today, sadly many have passed on. I recall Percy Edwards, a regular performer of his bird songs, before he was nationally famous. Locally there was Joe White, the singing bus driver; his favorite song was the Donkey Serenade. Other Ipswich performers were Eddie Parsons a brilliant banjo player and "Sore eyes" Bilner who was a regular performer on the piano

accordion. There were also many visiting performers from the armed forces who were stationed locally. These were wonderful evenings during a time when people enjoyed each other's company and we had to make our own entertainment. I wonder if there are any performers still around that were performing in those days."

"Of course the celebrations that took place at the end of hostilities were a very busy time for me. I remember coming home late one night from playing at a concert in town – someone had

The flags were flying at the Morland Road, for this Victory in Europe party. You can make out all the different nationalities depicted on the flags as they move.

dragged a piano out into Pickwick Road the next street to my home. They saw me arrive home and asked me to play; it was a very early morning when we finished. I also played at many street parties and remember arriving at a hall in Beaconsfield Road on my 3/6d black enameled bike which I left outside – no need to chain it up in those days! I kept up my love of playing music all my life. The first band I played with in 1945 was "the Swing Four" and our first engagement was at the Trimley Memorial Hall where there was a 40s dance on April 9 almost sixty years to the day since I played there as a fresh faced young chap. I played with the Grovenor Swingtette and the Mervyn Dale Dance Band in the 1950s and I still play – I enjoy an evening of reminiscing with those lovely songs of yesteryear – music that will live forever!"